WHERE DO WE GO FROM HERE?

WHERE DO WE GO FROM HERE?

An Inside View of Life in a Mental Health Hospital

Bethany Hacker

Cherish
EDITIONS

First published in Great Britain 2021 by Cherish Editions
Cherish Editions is a trading style of Shaw Callaghan Ltd & Shaw
Callaghan 23 USA, INC.
The Foundation Centre
Navigation House, 48 Millgate, Newark
Nottinghamshire NG24 4TS UK
www.triggerhub.org
Text Copyright © 2021 Bethany Hacker

British Library Cataloguing in Publication Data
A CIP catalogue record for this book is available upon request
from the British Library
ISBN: 978-1-913615-17-8
This book is also available in the following eBook formats:
ePUB: 978-1-913615-18-5

Cover design by Bookollective
Typeset by Lapiz Digital Services

To all those suffering with mental illness as well as those who don't understand it.

To my dad, who passed away before he could see me become a published writer… I hope he'd be proud.

Lastly, to those who just want something random to read or glance at while commuting to work and don't want to make eye contact with anyone.

CONTENTS

About the Author   ix
Preface   xi

Chapter One   3
Chapter Two   25
Chapter Three   57
Chapter Four   69
Chapter Five   83
Chapter Six   109
Chapter Seven   127
Chapter Eight   139
Chapter Nine   147

Acknowledgements   153

ABOUT THE AUTHOR

Bethany Hacker was born in Italy to American parents who worked as teachers on a US military base. She spent her developmental years there and ended up moving to the US for university, where she studied Political Science. After deciding that Europe felt more like home, she moved back to Italy and then on to the UK, where she was treated for various mental health issues. She currently works at a charity, helping families who have children in hospital, while gaining skills toward eventually becoming a therapist to help others cope with mental illness.

PREFACE

Regardless of where you are from, the story doesn't change. It is for everyone, and it is based upon my experiences in a private psychiatric hospital. I've tried hard not to change too much (especially the offbeat bits, as those are where the real story lies!), but all names and some situations have been changed to provide anonymity.

PART ONE

LIFE AT LAMPSTEAD

CHAPTER ONE

Monday, 8:52am

I wake up and through my blurry vision, see a nurse standing above me with a plastic cup of water and an even smaller paper cup with my morning meds. I briefly glance at it (I'd been given the wrong ones before), swallow, groggily say thanks, and fall back into my pillow and a deep sleep. Normal routine. What's normal you may ask? Nothing is. It is one of those indefinable words. After many weeks of missing my morning meds (I failed to climb out of my bed and zombie walk to the meds station – too much work), the nursing staff realized that they had to bring them to me. Meds in bed. Can't get better than that!

At first, I felt special, but now it is just normal. It is normal now for me to walk into the bathroom and have the lights turn on automatically. It is normal to take a shower and suddenly experience scalding water followed by ice cold water within a minute before returning to a somewhat normal temperature. It is also normal for that shower to turn off every five minutes until I wave my hand over the sensor. Heaven forbid there be a water faucet that I can turn on or a light switch that I can touch. I could drown, scald or scrape myself to death. I can't even have a towel hook, just in case I decide to hang all 5'10" of myself. I don't think any normal hook in a room slightly taller than me would support my weight and height.

Normal also means that if I need anything considered "dangerous", I have to ask, like for my hair straightener, razor blades and any cords involved with charging electronics, and then hand them back when finished. Never mind the fact that there is an iron in the laundry room and cords provided for me attached to the TV and lamps. I, along with many others, just happened to always "forget" to return them and no one followed up. Fine, most of the time... a few razor incidents... but I see that this lack of supervision could be dangerous for others. I think I'm abnormal living in a supposedly normal place – abnormal in the fact that my devious mind still works, though it is slightly warped.

Two years ago, I would have thought that anyone who lived this way was crazy. Now I think everything is normal. This is my life – Bethany Hacker, Room 77, inpatient at Lampstead Hospital. Admitted for depression, suicidal ideation, intentional overdoses, eating disorder, alcohol abuse, deliberate self-harm (DSH), and possible borderline personality disorder. Nothing seems crazy anymore, and at this moment in time, nothing I hear surprises me.

This morning I know that, as usual, something else will be a part of my normal daily routine. At some point today I will be asked one of my many dreaded questions.

"So, where are you from?" (It's a seemingly easy question to ask and answer.)

"I was born in Italy." (Here is where it gets complicated.)

"Why do you have an American accent?" *Not again – not this question again.* I breathe deeply and take a drag of my cigarette.

And thus, my day has begun. Today is a Monday. Most people dread Mondays, but I love them. I can't wait to see all of the therapists again and return to my normal weekly routine. I can honestly say that I love most of the therapists. I feel that they are like a big family. *My* family – a very twisted one of which I know very little about but they know all my deepest, darkest secrets.

Mondays also mean that there are things to do. Sundays are awful. Those of us who are depressed become even more so and struggle to find a reason to get out of bed. There is absolutely nothing to do here on a Sunday, unless you enjoy counting the pieces in the many boxes of puzzles available to entertain us in order to ensure that they are all there (yes, I have done that).

A Monday here at Lampstead is like the light at the end of a tunnel. No, that is too cliché, even for me. A Monday is like finding that sock you thought the

dryer ate a year ago. Finally, you have more options
for what you can put on your feet and where your feet
can take you. Don't get me wrong, it is wonderful when
the weekends have a great nursing staff working. At
least there are people to talk to and to have fun with.
However, these weekends aren't a common occurrence.

I have already missed breakfast. That's nothing
unusual. That's actually normal. I don't think I could
even tell you what they serve for breakfast. Even
though I have been here for so long, I have never
made it down to the dining room in the morning.
You are a special person if you get more than a grunt
from me before 10am. Even getting into groups in the
morning can be downright distressing.

*Ok, Beth, it's 9:45am. Are you going to support group? If
so, then you better get your ass downstairs to have a quick smoke
before you, yet again, tell everyone how empty and low you are
feeling today.*

I enter the room, sit in one of the chairs arranged in
a slightly misshapen circle and fill in the sign-in sheet.

Name: Bethany Hacker
Consultant: Dr Ramsey
Ward: Upper Court

The support group begins with the facilitator (therapist)
reminding everyone to turn their phones off and that
the group will run for 45 minutes. She/he has no

specific agenda and it is up to us to use the space to talk about whatever we want to, or to ask questions of the other members. Most importantly, we are reminded that what we hear and say here stays here. Yeah, yeah, yeah – what happens in Vegas stays in Vegas. It's all a load of bullshit. Nothing but gossip happens at Lampstead. We all know that that isn't always the case. We have nothing better to do with ourselves than to talk about others, as unkind as that sounds.

So we begin to introduce ourselves and say how we are feeling. My turn comes too quickly. "Hey. I'm Bethany, and I'm feeling a bit empty and low this morning." After that, I sit quietly, try and listen to what the others are saying and count down the minutes until the end of the group.

The problem with being here for so long (compared to many other patients) is that they come and go within a few weeks, and yet I stay. I have pretty much heard it all – well you never know I guess... You have the newcomers who barely talk, and when they do speak, they ask questions about the hospital. Then there are the people who have been here for about two weeks and think that they have been here forever and are sharing all sorts of new revelations that they have recently had. Some are just angry about not being "cured" yet. (What is the definition of cured when having a mental illness?)

Finally, there are those who are about to be discharged and are anxious about going out into "the real world", but nevertheless, they will keep in touch with everyone they have met here forever and ever because we share such a common bond. It's true, yet out in the real world it is easy to forget the bond. It is always the same. I have heard it all before and I am tired of it.

God Bethany, you are so jaded. You need to develop more compassion because at one point – a very, very long time ago – you were going through the exact same phases and ways of thinking. Stop feeling sorry for yourself and feeling like you are too screwed up to be taking up space here for so many months on an acute ward in a psychiatric hospital.

I wish I had the courage to tell everyone what I am thinking but I don't want to hurt already damaged egos and I really don't want to appear to be a "know it all". So, I sit quietly and offer encouragement when I can. Encouragement is easy, yet hard to give out. I *know* all the correct sayings and advice but have been too stubborn to be able to implement them on myself.

10:45am.

I run out of the room for another cigarette.

Don't talk to me. I want to stay in my little smoking corner by myself without anyone around. I am in an antisocial mood (this happens from time to time without knowing why) and the last thing I want right now is for someone to think that I am standing alone because I am lonely, instead of just being alone and enjoying my solitude. People here think that if you are alone you obviously must need attention. That is, until they have been here long enough to realize not to bother those on their own because it just becomes common knowledge. Oh God. Someone is coming. I've never seen this person before. Please don't talk to me and please don't ask me the other question.

"So, where are you from?"

"Mexico," I reply, as I stub out my half-smoked cigarette and walk away. *Shit. I just wasted half a cigarette. Cigarettes are like money here.*

One of the problems that come from being here for so long is that I have been to almost every group offered to patients that applies to me. Obviously I am not going to go to the OCD group or bipolar group since neither are problems for me. *Wow! I can identify two things that aren't wrong with me!*

I am pretty sure that I could lead most of the groups by now. I've been here long enough and have gone to many of them about 50 million times. If only they would give me the chance to at least lead the arts and crafts group. Oh wait! I'm not allowed scissors! There goes that plan, as well as so many others...

Caffeine is what I need. Caffeine will give me the boost I need to try and be social, and possibly even a bit witty. Instead of going to the free tea and coffee machine offered to patients, I head to my room, chug down a sugar-free Red Bull, and I am ready for the rest of the day. Well, not really, since caffeine doesn't do much for me anymore. Technically we aren't allowed caffeine (which is why I bypassed the caffeine-free coffee) but no one really abides by that rule – not even the staff. Actually, I'm not even allowed cans since I could potentially use the edges to cut myself (well, I have done that, so I suppose they have a point). Oh well. I kind of screwed myself on that one despite the fact that I could easily go into the rubbish bin and find a can.

11:30am.
I guess I will head to the Loss and Bereavement group. Ugh! I hate this group.

Same story. I enter the room, sit in one of the chairs arranged in another slightly odd circle and fill in the sign-in sheet.

Name: Bethany Hacker
Consultant: Dr Ramsey
Ward: Upper Court

"Hi. I'm Bethany and I am coming to this group because my key worker said I should but also because I think I suffer from a loss of identity and from major abandonment issues." Like I said, it's the same story. Yet this time it's different people and different losses.

I still cringe sometimes when I hear some of their stories. Some are so horrific that I can't believe that they have gotten through life for this long. I feel honoured to hear their struggles. Honoured by the fact that they are comfortable enough to share everything with a room full of strangers. If I had such a horrific past, I don't know if I could do it. These are some courageous people.

I shouldn't be here. I haven't suffered any major traumas in my life. I've had it easy. Everything I have ever wanted has been given to me. These are the people that need the help. These are the people who should be given the opportunity to be here as long as I have. I am just taking up space. Someone else should be sitting in this seat instead of me. I am truly selfish and worthless and don't deserve any of this. Fuck me... tears are close to coming out of my eyes. Nope. Not going to happen.

Before I know it, the group is over. I realize that I spent half of it criticizing myself. Sadly, this is normal.

1:00pm.
Lunchtime.
Nope, cigarette time instead. At least I have a bit of time outside alone before everyone comes out of lunch for an after-meal smoke. It's not that I don't enjoy the company of others (well, I'm starting to...) but I am just tired of meeting people, telling them my story and then having them leave.

No. I will not start thinking about my abandonment issues. I can't. I won't. There will be no crying today about long-lost friendships and what could have been. Why does she not talk to me anymore? How did I ruin her life? And so on...

I am also extremely tired of small talk. I have run out of things to say. The turnover of patients here is so frequent that my small talk conversations tend to repeat themselves.

People start coming out of the door after eating and I know that the dining room is closing. Oh well, no lunch for me today. I have probably seen the dining room at lunchtime only a few times more than I have been to breakfast. To do the math for you, that is probably about once or twice a month. I'm quite sure that some of the staff will notice that I didn't have breakfast or lunch, but I think they have given up trying to force me to eat. In the end, it really is my choice to nourish myself or not. Live or die. My choice.

I'm really hungry. I need to eat. I can't. I can't take the chance that I will gain weight. I have a hard time believing people when they tell me that I am thin. That's not possible. I have never been thin in my life and never will be. I'm just fat and ugly and nothing will change this fact of life.

I want to eat, though. I really want to. I want to eat so badly without thinking about what I am doing, like I believe that others can. It just seems impossible. I feel like crying. My brain is having a battle with itself and neither side seems to be winning… it is just being worn out. I am so tired of this. Tired of not being able to share a carefree meal with others. I am also to the point that although I am hungry, no food even sounds remotely good. I'm screwed.

2:00pm.

I take myself into the Relationships Level Two group.
I must have done this group about 50 million times
(and no, I don't think that I am exaggerating) but I
still get slightly anxious walking through the doors
and sitting in the circle. I can recite everything the
therapists are going to say, yet the meaning behind
the words still makes me think about my life. I have
trouble in relationships – relationships with myself,
friends, family, and pretty much everything that
lives or is tangible. This group should be renamed
'Relationships: How to avoid becoming Bethany – that
crazy one who has been here forever.' Yes, that is a
ridiculous name, but hey, I'm in the loony bin, you
can't expect wonders from me.

I try to find a chair that is out of the main eyesight
of the therapists leading the group. One of them is
my individual therapist, and I know she just waits for
the perfect moment to call me out and ask how I feel
about what she is saying. I begrudgingly sign in.

Name: Bethany Hacker
Consultant: Dr Ramsey
Ward: Upper Court

*Shit! Why can't my memory be better?! I can't remember
anything! Today's topic is sexuality. This is always awkward!
No. I will not look up and make eye contact. No. No. No.*

CRAP! I made eye contact with Laura, my therapist, or Lori whom I respect so much.

"Bethany! Will you please name one positive and one negative association with the word 'sexuality'?"

There is no way I am getting out of this one. HELP!

I keep my cool and casually answer with the words "exciting" and "exposed". To everyone else in the group, I think that I appear to not be bothered by the question. Only Laura knows what is really going on in my mind. She knows me better than I know myself. It is like she can read my mind before the thoughts have even entered my brain. She is so amazing that it is slightly terrifying. I know by her look that my answer doesn't satisfy her expectations, and yet she moves on.

The rest of the session moves slowly, or it could be possible that the clock just doesn't like me and decides to stop every time I look at it. *(Ok, I will not be accused of being paranoid as well!)* But, as I was expecting, we discuss our first times having sex, how we first learned about it, how we first learned about it, how our parent's sexual lives appeared to us when we were younger and how that may have had an effect on our relationships and sex in the present. We even start to get into talking about what is an appropriate or an inappropriate touch, gaze and speech.

Apparently all of this has affected us. As usual in this group, many patients take umbrage to what is being said. For example, some of the women don't believe that their possibly exposing relationships with their dads or other male family members at an early age has had any effect on their relationship with men now that they are older. Others think it is perfectly normal to have everyone in their families walk around the house naked.

According to the therapists, we are pretty much fucked up when it comes to relationships due to these and other behaviours. Some stories shared by patients who are, yet again, in the category of being the extremely brave, tell stories that are hard to hear and make me feel angry and upset about what has happened to them. I also question many of the ideas and theories that the therapists tell us, but this group isn't long enough to even start asking my questions. Not only do I feel too embarrassed to say some things out loud but I also know that I will get a more personalized answer when I ask Laura about it in my individual session.

3:30pm finally arrives.
Once again, I walk speedily out of the door until I realize that I have nowhere to rush to other than outside for another cigarette. My groups are over for the day and ironically the long hours await me before I can take my sleeping medication to go to bed.

So, what to do, what to do? The choices seem endless, which are very much unlike my energy levels.

I am emotionally exhausted today. I am emotionally exhausted after most days. Not everyone understands how tiring depression, anxiety and suicidal ideation are, and on top of that, how exhausting talking about your feelings about those issues makes you physically and mentally feel. I decide to take a nap.

Bethany! You should not be napping! You will never get well if you are constantly sleeping! You need to do something productive, or even better, communicate with people and be in the presence of others.

I choose to ignore the Drill Sergeant voice in my head and just sleep. After all, how can I be productive if I am too tired to do anything? I immediately fall asleep cuddling my stuffed lion, Safari (yes, I still sleep with a stuffed animal and I'm guessing half the population still does to some extent as well!) and don't wake up until around 5:30ish. Thank goodness! Two hours have passed and I'm slightly closer to being able to go to bed for the night!

Cigarette time. I see the usual people out there. We are kind of like a smoking club. I say hi to those I know as I walk to my corner. They know that I like my space and that I have a specific place I like to smoke. I try to ignore the newbies that have joined our smoking club. They can be overly hyper or overly sad due to their diagnoses. Some are detoxing from drugs and alcohol, and a few are very new to Lampstead and simply look extremely nervous. There are also those who are adjusting to their new medications and the possible side effects, and they don't seem to know what to do with themselves or where to go – let alone who to talk to.

However, there is normally at least one person out there who provides me with a bit of entertainment. It sounds extremely horrible of me to laugh or find enjoyment in others' illnesses, but we do often get a lot of "characters" here at Lampstead.

Like I said, I think I am a bit jaded by everything happening here and try to get any laughs out of what I can in this extremely boring environment. So yes, I can be quite callous, but the more "crazy" you are, the more entertaining you can be to watch. I do try to "check myself" and make sure that I am still sensitive and don't turn my humour into judging. We are all here because of mental illnesses, but we don't all show them in the same way.

6:00pm.
Dinnertime… *sigh, I have to go into the dining room and eat or I will be in trouble – physically, mentally and with the staff. I hate getting in trouble. I still want to be the perfect child and patient.*

I walk down the slight slope of doom toward the dining room and look at the menu before entering.

Appetizer: Crostini topped with beets and goat's cheese. *Ok, that sounds halfway decent. I can do that.*

Main Course: baked cod in butter and lemon sauce. *Nope. No cod and definitely no butter.* Alternative Main: pork chops. *Why does it always have to be pork?* Vegetarian Option: tofu and lentils in a red pepper and tomato sauce. *Seriously? In other words that means a weird mix of random vegetables and soft tofu. It will take the form of some strange looking soup mix... ugh.*

Dessert: ? *I realize that I never even bother looking at what it is. I never intend to even look at the dessert, let alone eat it. That is definitely a no no. I have trained myself to not enjoy dessert. Ok... so I guess I will order a sandwich. Not a real meal but enough to satisfy my needs and everyone else's.*

I walk to the counter and order a ham, cheese and lettuce sandwich on brown bread from the incredibly handsome waiter, Pablo. Hey, just because I am in a mental hospital doesn't mean a girl can't dream!

I needn't really tell him or any of the other waiters what I want on my sandwich (or my occasional omelette). They all know what I am going to ask for. It's always the same – ham, cheese and the occasional peppers or onions. They, as well as every single staff member from the housekeeping and maintenance department to every therapist and nurse, know my name and always say hi and joke around with me in the hall. People seem to really enjoy talking to me, and like me and my personality. I honestly have no idea why. There really is nothing special about me – if anything, I am a pretty boring, meaningless person.

Seeing a couple of other Lampstead long timers, Jade and Claire, I walk over to the table to wait for my sandwich. They are always up for a good laugh, and when the three of us get together we are nothing but trouble. We are loud, boisterous and generally rude – especially to one another. Today we are talking about one of the new patients (not in a cruel way, I must add).

That is one benefit of having been here a long time. Jade and Claire have been here many months, yet still not as long as me. In a way, we have been here so long that nothing scares us and it's better to focus on the humour of our situations rather than dwell on the extremity of our own issues. When my sandwich arrives we are in the middle of counting the number of times a new patient wanders back and forth between the table and the buffet to get one small thing, such as a piece of bread, then another and then another. She continuously walks back and forth, but she is so slow that the wait staff think she has finished eating and take away her many small plates. Only we seem to notice that she is just taking one of her very slow walks back to the buffet. When she gets back to the table, the shocked look on her face makes us burst out laughing. She has no idea what has happened and begins her slow trek back to the buffet to start over again. I feel incredibly sorry for her and can't imagine what must be going on in her head.

Wow. I really hope that kind of thing never happens to me. To be honest, I don't want to be laughing. I feel sick inside. What in the world caused her to reach that point? I really shouldn't be here. Every reason I am here is self-inflicted, whereas it seems like she has no control. I choose to hurt myself and if I could just make the choice to stop doing all these things, I wouldn't be here taking up space. It's a choice. I want to hurt myself. I want to further burn my wrists and slice at my skin. I want this to be over. I want to take the selfish way out of this mess I have created, and kill myself.

People say suicide is for the weak, but you have to be brave. I want to be brave but there is still this glimmer of hope and fear inside me that prevents me. It's a very dangerous game I am playing with myself. I continuously push my limits to see how far I can go.

Yet another battle is going on in my head: to just do it, or suffer and live with these excruciating thoughts that make life seem unbearable. I know the rational answer, but my emotional answer is quite different and one that not many people seem to understand. It is a battle that is in the back of my head and has been there for as long as I can remember. It will probably never go away.

I need to get out of the dining room quickly, so as usual, I walk out for another smokey treat. My reward. My choice of a slower way to kill myself.

The manics seem to be on quite a high after dinner – as are those in the high state of their bipolar. I choose to stay away but make the mistake of entering the realm of the paranoids where I am accused of staring and talking badly about them (I'm not) and the people still detoxing continue to ask me for more and more cigarettes. I cave and give in. I can only hope that someone would do the same for me in that situation. I try to reassure the others that I am not looking at them and thinking bad things about them, but it doesn't seem to help. I quickly run away before things escalate.

I want to cry. I feel so alone. Why can't I cry? I need to cry. No one seems to understand me. Well, how could they if I don't even understand myself?

I flop down onto my bed and contemplate the rest of my evening. Distraction techniques and coping mechanisms. I guess I *have* learned something here. I choose to go into the lounge and work on my puzzle and possibly try to do a bit of knitting. Instead of being a 28-year-old going to a bar or the cinema (or whatever a 28-year-old does) for the evening. I am very slowly turning into an old lady. Next thing I know I'll be dozing in front of the TV with a puzzle piece in one hand and a cup of tea in the other.

8:00pm.
I am still sitting in the lounge when I hear the usual night staff parade in.

"Hi! We're the night staff! Here's Bethany, Room 77."

Aw, Deen is here – and there is his wink. He knows I find this part of the evening hilarious… the parade, the song and dance of the nurses… Here we go again.

Actually, it is pretty entertaining. Like we didn't know who you were already. Obviously you are the night staff. You weren't here this morning or throughout the day. I may be crazy, but I think I can notice the change in faces and if you aren't the staff, we are in big trouble as you are all holding our medicine charts and wearing name tags.

"Hi Bethany, I'm Henry."

"Hi Bethany. I'm Delilah."

"Hi Beth!"

On and on and on. I know exactly who all of these people are and they all know me!

"Hi, Brittany. How's my baby tonight?"

Ok, Wanda, I've known you for how many months now? How hard is it to remember that my name is Bethany?! Now I think she does it just to annoy me.

I manage to stay awake until 10:30pm so that I can take my night meds – one being a sleeping pill. The last thing for me to do is to take a shower to avoid having to wake up early in the morning. What should take about ten minutes turns into at least twenty minutes. I so very much love that my shower turns itself off after a few minutes. It is such a joy and a time saver to blindly try and find the "on" sensor for the shower whilst having soap in my eyes.

11:30pm.
Finally.

I crawl into bed and turn on my TV, then set the sleep timer for it to turn off after twenty minutes, though I know I will be asleep soon before that. I know that tomorrow will come sooner than I want it to, and I am already dreading it. *How to get through tomorrow, and the next day, and the next...*

11:45pm.
Sleep.

CHAPTER TWO

8:52am. Tuesday morning.
Repeat.
How the fuck did I get here, in this detrimental, scary place in my life?

March of 1986. Let's start there.
I was born.

There is nothing wrong with me having been born, but that's just where this story begins. It begins on a US military base in Italy. A mini American community within a large passionate country filled with a vibrant lifestyle. My future identity crisis can be traced back to this point in my life.

Issue number one: my parents are Americans who live on that military base, but they are not in the military. Issue number two: I am therefore American, yet I was born in Italy. Issue number three: the military base may be a mini US, but only in a few ways does it actually resemble the US.

Three more issues soon pop up. I learn that all the friends I make would move away every three years (welcome to my abandonment issues); I will never get to know any of my extended family in the US; and I will have to somehow find a way to "survive" in four types of communities: Italian, American, Military and family. My family community means only my mom and dad, since I am an only child. All of these factors helped to contribute to the Bethany who landed herself here in the Lampstead Hospital.

I'm an only child, so as expected, I fit the spoiled only-child stereotype. I was given everything I could ever want: the latest items in toys, clothes, accessories, electronics and everything that any kid could want. I attended an expensive university in the US. There was no real reason to go there other than it would look good on my résumé, as it was well known that I liked the location (close to NYC) and the campus was beautiful.

If I ever needed money, it was there for me. I only had to ask for it. I'm not saying that I didn't need a good reason to ask for money (the money would still be given to me no matter what, but I had to at least say why) – my dad was always giving me lectures on how to save money and invest it wisely. Sadly, I never listened to it. I now rely solely on their income, as I earn no money. I never listened to a lot of the advice my parents gave me, but to be fair, I never needed much advice. Well, I also never wanted it, but I think that I would have had to ask to get some advice, and therefore (since I'm stubborn) I never asked for it. I tended to do my own thing and somehow managed to never get in trouble. I was what one could call a "goody two shoes".

I never rebelled. I missed that phase of life when teenagers and freshmen in college went to wild parties, drank, did drugs, got tattoos, and slept around with random men. I'm not saying that any of that is technically "bad" or the "wrong" thing to do, but I never chose or really wanted to do any of those things. I didn't start drinking heavily until my senior year in college. To my own embarrassment, I didn't lose my virginity until 26. I feel humiliated to even say that. I still don't have any tattoos and have never been in a serious relationship. It was a huge deal when I got a second and third hole in my ear. I absolutely hate wild parties. I'd rather be in a bar/pub and have a few beers or wine (Prosecco in particular) and talk to a few people rather than raving and dancing and getting wasted in an incredibly social situation.

Instead of this "typical teenage lifestyle", I chose a less obvious way of rebellion much earlier in life. Body image and the way I saw myself – as well as the way others saw me – became a major focus for me around the age of eight or nine. I don't want to see it as a blame game or say that someone or something caused all my issues, though I do have several theories (you can't be in a psychiatric hospital for a long time without having a few ideas!). Kids don't just start hating their bodies with so much animosity for no reason.

At an early age, I began to compare myself to others and view myself in a negative way. As far as I know, every young kid goes through a "chubby" phase as they are growing into their new bodies. I definitely went through that phase, but between the ages of 8 and 12, a child doesn't know that it will pass. When I looked in the mirror, I was honestly horrified at the image looking back at me. I saw myself as a massive blob of fat with frizzy short hair and glasses. My clothes didn't help since I dressed in a baggy shirt to try and hide myself. Not only did I try to hide myself *from* myself, but I hid myself from others as well. I didn't want my parents to have to suffer with having an overweight child instead of a perfect, beautiful one.

I was also conscience that many kids my age were starting to make special relationships with others of the opposite sex. I hid myself from boys because I was afraid of the ridicule and disgust if they knew that I liked them. This insecurity did the opposite of what I wanted. Instead of being hidden in the background, the young boys did in fact make fun of me because I was so shy.

Nevertheless, I created a personality for myself; one of a very shy, unseen, nerdy, embarrassed girl who believed no one would like her because of how she looked or what she had to say. It is interesting to look back now and see how easy it was for me to fall into that particular personality as it became a part of my everyday life. It also didn't help that several of my "friends" took advantage of my low self-esteem and used it to boost their own through bullying. Well, I guess, who hasn't had that happen to them?

I'm thinking about all that I have learned here at Lampstead, and I realize that family plays such a huge part in how we grow up and who we become. Though I've been told this didn't happen, I remember that around the age of eight, my Dad would weigh me, and if I had lost a pound, he would give me a dollar. Dollars are great for kids with no income, but just stepping onto the scale put me into a panic... what if I had gained weight? What would be said then? I even remember trying to turn the scale backward so that it wasn't set at zero to start with. It gave me a bit of leeway. (I still have a fear of scales to this day.)

What also didn't help were the thoughts from my extended family. When I heard relatives (who I only saw in the summer) tell me how big I'd gotten, I had this warped view that they meant I'd gained weight. I realize now, or at least I hope, that they were saying that I was older and more grown up from when they'd seen me the year before. However, when I received a Barbie workout video from my grandparents for

Christmas, it only confirmed what I already thought to be true. I was overweight.

There were even comments from my dance teachers that I was getting a bit big... Plus, we always had to have mini physicals with the school nurse, and after weighing everyone, each kid almost always asked her to tell them what they weighed as a sort of competition. She seemed to respond to everyone's requests except mine. I asked her several times and she never answered. At that point, I thought she just didn't hear me, but I think she was protecting me from potential ridicule. I had no idea that my self-esteem at that early an age was only the tip of the iceberg.

It was around this time – the pre-teen years – that I started playing around with skipping meals and trying to throw up after eating. I can clearly remember turning on the shower after a meal and trying to eliminate all of the undesirable food (though I still found pleasure in eating). I was really bad at it because obviously it isn't something they teach you in school!

Luckily (well, looking back, probably unluckily), I am pretty sure that my parents didn't have any inkling about it. I even remember asking my mom to tell me bedtime stories where I was the main character. In some part of the story I told her to include a scene where I got incredibly badly hurt... Was this a very early version of thoughts of self-harm? I'm assuming that my parents still believed that I was the happy child they took to Florida every summer for vacation, the child who loved making sandcastles and walking along the beach looking for shells, the child who was so excited when she did her first underwater handstand. There was still a lot of that childhood excitement in me, but the self-loathing was very slowly beginning to fight its way to the forefront. That iceberg of self-hatred went deep into the icy depths of a lonely and forgotten sea.

Enough of that for now. Why do I keep dwelling on the past? Well, it's easier to do than to focus on the here and now, and it's definitely easier than feeling hope for the future.

Hope. Now that is a funny word. "Be hopeful!" Yeah, right. The people dying from cancer feel hopeful that a cure will be found. Anyone who is physically ill can feel hopeful for a positive outcome. Sometimes their hope becomes actuality and real, but this is due to other people fixing them or solving the problem. They have no control. So what am I hopeful for when I have no one but myself to help me choose hope? I have to hope to have hope. No one can do that for me.

Depression is a dreadful illness that affects your physical self as well as your mental self. Curing one (physical or mental) still leaves the other. The other self needs its buddy back for balance, and what was once "cured" is back with a vengeance. A cycle develops which requires something more powerful to destroy it — just like the only way to kill a vampire is with a wooden stake through the heart.

Nevertheless, the vampire probably created other vampires and you only killed the one. Depression does the same. Even if depression is defeated, you are still left with other issues – self-harm, alcohol, eating disorders, drugs. And the thoughts of the vampire – just like the thoughts of depression – stay with you. The thought of suicide remains in the background. It stays there like a bit of static on the radio that you just can't get rid of…

8:52am. Tuesday morning.
I don't have anything to do until 10:00am, but I purposely set my alarm for 8:52am. My snooze button goes off every eight minutes, so I figure I can hit it at least four times before I need to wake up (or at least somewhat wake up).

Somewhere in between those snoozes, the nurse comes in to give me my meds. I don't really remember it but I see the empty paper cup next to my bed and figure that it must have happened. I walk into my bathroom and thank God that my light turns on automatically because I'm still in a state of sleep and I doubt that I could have found the switch on my own. (Ok, I guess I am grateful for the fact that the builders of the hospital added that plan for the safety of the patients.) I change from my comfy PJs into a pair of slightly more appealing sweatpants and sweatshirt. I gave up long ago trying to be fashionable and wearing "real" clothes and make-up. This is a hospital, after all, and it's not like I am trying to impress anyone.

However, let us remember that this is a hospital of mixed genders. As the stereotype says, men need to have some desires met. Women walking around in what some would call pyjamas does not help the men in this world. We look like we are halfway in bed, just the way they need it (I learned this in an unfortunate way in the hospital… Let's just say that it is something I probably should have told the nurses and spoken up about in the Relationships group). Unluckily for me, many found my attire appealing.

Well, maybe it's not what I wear. Think positively, Bethany! I have to remember that these men have been here for a fairly long time as well, and any woman seems attractive to them!

After making myself a proper caffeinated coffee, I walk down the many stairs and twisted hallways to the outside smoking world. It is often said at Lampstead that if you don't smoke when you come in or even if you gave up a long time ago, you will definitely be a smoker once you leave. This is a very true statement.

First of all, it is something to do to relieve the boredom of sitting in your room or the lounge. It also gives you an opportunity for "fresh" air, and since so many people smoke here, the non-smokers find themselves alone in the building and come outside with their smoking friends to be social. They very soon try their first cigarette. I started smoking about five years ago, and I only smoked a few a day. Now that I am here, I smoke many, many more.

Wow. I don't think I can even put a number on how many I smoke a day. That's a bit scary! Oh no. I forgot the other question I dread being asked as someone starts to walk over. Come on, Beth. Smoke quicker! Quicker! Shit, too slow.

"Hi. I'm James."

"Bethany." *Here it comes now…*

"So, how long have you been here?"

I never want to scare the new people. Because undoubtedly, they will be here for a much shorter time, but my answer always freaks them out. "Just a few months."

Hmm, how many months have I been here? Is it eight now? I lost count after the four-month mark.

"Wow! That's an awfully long time."

"Yeah it is, but my insurance is amazing. I'll probably be out in the next two weeks or so."

Yup. I have started to lie to myself as well as to the other patients. But that's normal, I guess!

"Don't worry. You probably won't be here too long. Most people leave after about 28 days."

I really don't want to tell him that it is because their insurance doesn't always cover more than that, even if they still aren't feeling much better. I hate seeing people panic as their insurance runs out and they aren't ready to face the outside world yet. I am so incredibly lucky. Why am I so lucky to have such amazing insurance? I surely don't deserve it!

"It's really great to meet you, James but I'm sorry,

I have to go see my individual therapist now for a session. I'll see you around!"

At least what I am saying is the truth. I do have to go and see Laura as it is nearly 10:00am. I walk slowly to the waiting room and take a seat until I am called up. Several other people are waiting to see their therapists as well. One is crying. One is looking extremely nervous. *This must be her first session. Poor girl. I hope she can get through it.* Most of the others appear to be just like me: silently waiting and trying not to make eye contact.

It's best to focus on yourself before meeting your therapist. You need to go up and have something to say, or at least know how you are feeling at this particular moment or you will be screwed and not get much out of the session if you either lie or have no idea as to how you are.

10:05am.
"Hi Bethany! Sorry I'm a bit late. I couldn't find the room key." *Normal.* "Shall we go up?"

Why does she have to walk up the stairs so quickly? I really should have eaten more last night for energy. Never mind. I know I wouldn't have even if I had to run a marathon today. Food is food, and food scares me.

"Ok. Here we are. Room 15. Have a seat and I'll look for my name tag to put outside the room so people know we are in here."

Umm… which chair do I sit in? I've been in this room before, but I can never remember which one is mine. Having had a bit of previous therapy training, I choose the seat under the clock so that she can see the time.

I hate this but I know it's how it should be. I just want to see what time it is so that I know how long I have left without having to obviously turn my head to see the clock. I don't want her to think that she is boring me, but I need to know when to start wrapping up my conversation. I need to feel a bit in control of the situation.

I know what she would say if she knew what was going through my head. "But Bethany, why do you care what I think? Why do you think it would bother me for you to know what time it is? You are still in a childlike state that fears getting in trouble and doesn't want someone to get upset with you. You have a right to state your demands."

She walks back in and sits down in the chair, bringing with her a pillow that she puts behind her back.

This is a test, and at least today I am ready for it and remember what it is. I need a pillow to hold onto during our sessions for comfort and she knows this. Last session I didn't have one but there was one on her chair. Halfway through the session she asked me why I didn't ask her for it. My reply was that I didn't want to bother her and thought she may have needed it. Right away she challenged me and reminded me that I still have a choice to ask just as she has the choice to say no. I have learned that it is all about choices... I am ready this time.

"Laura can I please have the pillow?"

"Of course. Why did you ask?"

"Because I wanted it."

And also I knew that you would kindly chastise me if I didn't ask. She knows me too well. It's a good thing I know. That is her job!

"Hi."

"Hi," she replies. I know the routine by now, but it terrified me in our first few sessions. She stares at me for as long as it takes for me to say something.

"So... umm... yesterday was ok. Nothing really happened." *Umm. What else is there to say?* "I'm still feeling quite low and my suicidal thoughts are still there. The weekend wasn't so great, though. I slept almost all day on Sunday because I couldn't think of a reason to get out of bed. I did try and stay awake, and I did get out of bed and go downstairs for a cigarette a few times."

I slightly cringe at saying this because she hates the fact that I smoke. Once, she even took my cigarette box away from me and refused to give it back. Yes, I am still slightly angry about that because those things cost me quite a bit of money!

"However, when I was awake and actually thinking

and conscious, I started ruminating about all sorts of stuff. Like how ashamed I am about still being here, the fact that I don't have any friends, how worthless I feel and what a waste of space I am, how hopeless I feel, how no one seems to understand me, and all sorts of things like that. I especially thought about killing myself and how easy it would be to just do so. Just run out to the shops in-between my 15 minute checks and get as many over-the-counter meds as I can and as much alcohol as I can and just sleep my pain away. So easy. It would be so easy."

"So why don't you?"

I think about this for a while. It's not like I haven't done this before. I have gone out and gotten meds and alcohol and been taken to the actual hospital because of it. But I haven't done enough to permanently hurt myself. I never took enough, but every time I end up playing this precarious game of life and death.

"Well, at the moment I don't want to get anyone in trouble. It would be the staff that is taking over my care that would get in trouble for not watching me closely enough. However, I am a little bit scared about impulsivity."

I have a history of being impulsive with self-harming and overdosing. I know that I don't even trust myself.

"All I want to do is do as much harm to myself as I can. I don't think people believe me, but my impulse to kill myself is getting much stronger day by day. Why can't people understand how I'm feeling? They all seem to think that I'm ok and just a generally happy person. It makes me feel so… angry, I guess. I just feel so overemotional and so fucking upset and no one knows."

Laura nods her head and lets me know that she understands and knows how depressed I am. She lets me know that she is here for me (and all that jazz).

I continue to talk about all that's on my mind at the moment and how shitty I am feeling, though I'm not really feeling too interested in this session and she can tell. It kind of feels like I never find anything positive to say and continue to say the same things. Like I said before, she knows me.

No, it's not that I'm not interested; I think that I am just so tired of emotions. I'm just tired of everything. I want to go to bed.

She goes on and on and I listen. She tells me that she is angry that I'm not eating and that I haven't been to any AA meetings. This hurts. I hate being a disappointment to someone who I admire so much. Despite my seemingly non-interest in all that I say, it is an emotional session and I know I will be affected afterwards.

She puts in her two cents about what she thinks is best for me and I just feel so emotionally drained from talking and listening. I have a love/hate relationship with my sessions with her. I love that she cares so much and that I can talk openly and honestly and actually be understood, but I often feel low or extremely overwhelmed at the end of the 50 minutes.

10:55am.
Our session ends and I ask for a hug, which she gives me. It was a big step for me when I asked for my first hug. I really just needed some human contact and to just be held. I think I started crying that first time. I still just need to be held. No, need isn't a strong enough word for what I feel. Crave is better. I am so incredibly drained. I think I need some diazepam.

11:15am.
After my 5mg of diazepam, I head down again for... guess what? Yes! You are correct! A cigarette! Only this time, I head out to the front garden... fewer people, more open space. I probably should have gone to my Drama therapy group at 11:00am, but at the moment I don't think that I have the mental capacity today to deal with that group *(mental capacity – Ha! I'm in a mental hospital! If I had a proper mental capacity, I wouldn't be here!)*.

Drama therapy is not what it sounds like. There is no acting. There are no scripts or props and there definitely are no costumes. They should probably rename the group... I know a lot of people who are scared to go because they don't want to act. In reality, more drama happens in the corridors of the hospital and in the smoking garden than in any of the groups. If you want to get something out of this group, you need to walk into Drama therapy with an open and receptive mind. The extremely talented, grounded and compassionate therapist Sarah leads this group, and she "invites" you to try activities within the space instead of telling you what to do.

That unto itself involves a challenge. You have to actually make a choice: only you can decide if you accept the invitation or not. The group requires you to be open and vulnerable to whatever emotion you may be feeling at any given moment. This is why I chose not to go after my therapy session with Laura. I am too emotionally drained and vulnerable to actually concentrate on any other emotions that may pop up.

I also feel quite guilty about not going because I know today's topic would be especially relevant to me. The topic for today is "your shadow aspect" – so basically, the inner demons that are a driving force for most of the people at the hospital. I know that this group will bring up a lot of sad and depressing feelings, and although I still need to explore my demons, I just can't today. I can't write a letter to my inner child. I can't use toys – *well I guess toys are props* – to represent my family and those who have been involved in my life. I definitely can't sit in a chair in front of the entire group and have a discussion with myself. This would require me to "become" my shadow aspect – in my case, these aspects would be self-loathing, hatred and the worthlessness that I feel about myself – and talk as if I was this all-encompassing demon. I would have to say why these aspects are in my life and how (as the shadow aspect) I help Bethany. I'm already feeling impulsive today and feel like harming myself, so I really don't need the extra depressing thoughts invited into my head.

Hmm. Thinking of harm, I do have several boxes of paracetamol collected and stored up in my closet… I could take a mini overdose… No! Beth! This is only a temporary feeling and it will pass. Plus, the longer I wait, the more boxes I will have collected in my room for the real deal…

12:00pm.
I've been caught up in my thoughts and smoking cigarettes for about 45 minutes now. It's sometimes still hard to believe that I can waste so much time so easily. Well, it helps that it's a sunny day without a cloud in sight, and no one has walked up to me to ask some horrid question whilst I've been sitting on the bench.

I actually walk into the dining room to see what's for lunch and see if anyone I'd like to talk to is sitting down. Nope.

Well hey, I can say I tried, right? If anyone asks, I'll just say that I had a sandwich. No big harm in that lie. Only harm to myself. Though I kind of wish that more attention would be placed on this issue. I really need to be pushed because I know I need serious help. They've given up though. Although I know it is my choice, I think that maybe I just want attention. Now that makes me feel guilty. How dare I need so much attention!

12:30pm.

I walk into the dim, grungy lounge with my book.
I may as well make use of my time before my
next group.

*Why are there no windows in here? Why is there no air?
What is that smell? I don't even want to know what that stain
is on the pillow.*

I open my book to where I left the marker a few
days ago and start to try and read. I used to be an avid
reader – I used to be able to finish several books in a
week, but I know I won't be able to read more than a
few pages now. I am so tired…

1:45pm.

I wake up to knocking on my bedroom door. It is
Zoe, wondering if everything is ok.

"Yeah," I say groggily, as she closes the door. *Where
am I? What happened? Why is the window on the right side of
my bed instead of the left? Oh yeah…*

I look up and see the credits rolling from the *Friends*
DVD. I must have moved into my bedroom and put
on the TV before I fell asleep. Waking up here still
jolts me sometimes. One would think that after eight

months (or more) of being in the hospital, sleeping on the same bed would become "normal".

Nope. I still wake up and wonder where I am. I scare myself, but I'm blaming that on the medication that I am taking. *It can't be me. I'm not that crazy to not even know my surroundings.*

1:55pm.
I go out for a quick smoke and I run up to my group in the yellow room – Anger Management.

Wow, I am feeling extremely lightheaded. It definitely can't be that I haven't eaten, the nap, the exhaustion of running up the stairs or the cigarette. I'll blame that on my drugs as well.

My first week here, I was given my personalized schedule for which groups would suit me best. My key worker, Grace (who would soon turn into a person I greatly respect, admire and trust), scheduled me in for Anger Management on Tuesday afternoons. *What?! Why in the world do I need anger management? I honestly can't remember ever yelling at anyone in my entire life and think I've only gotten into a few mini arguments. I am not an angry person.*

I did question her on why she added it to my schedule, and her answer was that anger is an extremely healthy emotion and that if we don't feel it, there is a reason for not feeling it. Ok, I'll give her credit for that. I don't usually enjoy being wrong, but she definitely deserves kudos for putting me in the group.

Today's group is filled up with the usual attendees and a few new faces. I know that many of them have the same reaction toward anger that I still struggle with. I have to push myself to get angry with people and situations that I would normally just shrug off. But you know, it is ok to be angry if someone (even accidentally) drops and breaks your favourite mug, or if another person cuts in front of you as you are driving. It's healthy. In the group they like to say that depression comes from repressed anger. It completely makes sense. Maybe if I had been able to actually express my anger at a younger age, I wouldn't be as depressed as I am now. *You can't start getting yourself into the "what ifs", Beth. Keep it in the here and now.*

This group starts a bit differently than many of the others. After introducing ourselves we talk about things that have made us angry within the past week. When I first started coming to the group, I never had an answer to the question. Aileen, the therapist, of course had a counter argument for me saying I don't get angry.

"If you don't get angry with others, do you get angry at yourself?"

She has entered the part of my mind that I like to keep hidden. "Yes, I do, for almost everything." My wrists and arms looked as though I had struggled to run away from rabid dogs in the middle of the woods. Burn marks and cuts everywhere. She pointed these out to me and said that these clearly visual *mutilations* mean that I most definitely have anger inside of me.

Since that first meeting I try my best to go back to the group, although it often bores me since I have been to it so many times already. Aileen has apparently noticed a difference in me since I have been able to openly say whatever has angered me. I see it in myself as well. I often find myself kicking things, ranting and raving about events, and more verbally expressing myself to Laura. Occasionally, I'd get some apples from the canteen saying that I would eat them but instead I would throw them against the outside fence.

However, I did go through a phase where my mostly contained anger turned against me. I started forcefully punching the cement walls in my room, which not only scared some of the other patients but caused swollen knuckles and possibly mini fractures here and there.

I haven't done that in a while. My knuckles aren't swollen as much anymore. Maybe I should give it another try. After all, it isn't as self-destructive as cutting or burning…

Today's session is one that always amuses me. We have to draw an image that represents our anger. I always choose to draw a giant-sized Pac-Man eating all the dots and whatever gets in its way. It has become more and more detailed the more I go to this group. We also have to say words that could represent anger in the form of nature, colour, sound and smell (to name a few). I thought today's session would be the same: earthquake; red, roaring noise; ash blanketing the background, but instead we had a new one.

Good ol' Matt. He always, without a doubt, makes me laugh. The room was completely silent until he opened his mouth and compared anger to having diarrhoea. It's extremely painful, loud and uncontrollable: like burning lava spitting out of a volcano with an intoxicating smell. There is no release until the anger (or, in this case, the diarrhoea) has been let out. Much to Aileen's chagrin, the group couldn't stop laughing throughout the entire group. Probably one of my favourite Anger Management groups ever!

3:30pm.
Matt and I walk down to the smoking garden together, still laughing with tears running down our faces. Matt is now a day-patient, so he doesn't have to endure the endless boring nights here. He used to be like me – a fellow inmate at Lampstead Hospital; however, due to insurance and the fact that he began to manage life well on his own, he comes in for group sessions but is allowed to leave with no consequences. I am incredibly jealous of his achievements, though it is always wonderful to see him. He also gives the best hugs in the world, and sometimes a hug is all you

need to lift your mood a bit. We talk a bit about our week, and before he leaves for the day we give each other words of wisdom as well as the habitual, "Call if you need anything." *Yay! Another hug!*

4:00pm.
As I am walking back to my room, one of the slightly elderly millionaires who occasionally pops in for a mental health "top up", stops me and tells me to wait. He comes back with a photo of a horse. He says that she is a young filly racehorse who is without a name and has decided to name her Bethany because of me. I take it as quite the compliment coming from him, and quite frankly, I'm shocked. I never knew that I could have such an impact on someone. It just goes to show that you never know what the small things you do can add up to. *I am choosing to carefully ignore the fact that somehow I remind him of a horse... but hey, how many people can say that they have had a racehorse named after them? This is a horse that I shall be betting on in the future!*

4:30pm.
Nap time!

6:00pm.
I let out a moan as yet another nurse tries to wake me up. *I thought I was here because I am very vulnerable and have a fragile mental state. Isn't waking me up from my*

very deep (and much needed) sleep counterproductive to my wellbeing? I'm doing something to nurture myself. I am just following the rules! All the nurses and therapists are always telling us that we should be nurturing ourselves on a daily basis, and here is Michelle, waking me up!

"Beth! It's dinnertime! Are you going down to dinner?"

I mutter something that I think sounds something like "no" and hope that she leaves me alone so I can snuggle deeper into my covers. This normally works and gives them the clear indication that I will stubbornly refuse if anyone tries to get me up. This doesn't work with Michelle, though. She knows me too well. I've only known her for the eight months of *this* admission, though I feel as though she has been a part of my life since the beginning of my Lampstead adventure. She proceeds to pull the covers off me (thank God I have clothes on) and drags me out of bed.

"Get yourself down to dinner. I know I can't force you to eat, but I can at least make sure you get down to the dining room."

Ugh. I love and hate her at this moment. I go down and order my special omelette, then take it back up to my room. At least this way they won't know if I eat the whole thing or not and I don't have to sit and socialize with people.

I'm still groggy from the whole ordeal and just want to get under the covers, but I take a bite of my pizza-shaped egg mash up and I'm instantly awake. *Wow!*

This is amazing! Why did I hesitate to eat this? This must be the world's best omelette, or I am much hungrier than I thought. Yeah, it is probably the latter.

I quickly scoff down the food like a zombie eats a body. *I think I've been watching too many horror movies in here because all the examples that come to my mind involve some kind of fanciful creature.*

I'm tired. Really tired. I know that I have to socialize though. I will be chastised if I end up spending all day and night in my room. I want to be around people at the moment for the sole reason being that my mind is starting to go to that deep dark scary place that I can't always control. It's a state of mind when I know that I'm more prone to impulsive behaviour. *There is a lightbulb in that lamp. Easy to break and sharp glass edges. You also have those scissors hidden away, Beth. Where are they again? Oh yeah, behind my books. And there is always the opportunity to run to the shop and grab anything or everything if I want to... Anything I want to... Ok, Bethany. You can do something in 30 minutes if you want to. Just 30 minutes. In the meantime, go to the lounge. Yes! Go!*

I hate this stupid brain of mine. Why is it that I have to torture myself? What have I actually done that is so bad that I feel the need to punish myself so harshly? *Stop ruminating Bethany! Get your big fat ass into the lounge!* I really am a nice person. I'm just a bully to myself.

I walk into the lounge, and I am grateful to see people in there watching some random reality TV show.

I sit and stare at the screen and listen to some of the idle chitchat of other patients and the occasional yelling at the screen as some celebrity does something predictably idiotic. The next thing I know, 30 minutes has turned into a few hours. It's amazing how easy it is to distract yourself even if you don't want to intentionally do so. I have to give credit to the therapists for this piece of advice. Distraction techniques are amazing tools to develop. I could have gotten myself into a lot of dangerous situations tonight, but I didn't. Well I can check off one more day to my list of days I have gotten through without hurting myself in some way. These periods of time don't usually last very long, but I guess every day I get through is a good one.

11:00pm.
Meds, a somewhat quick shower, then bed.

Childlike innocence is wonderful... until you grow out of it and realize you are in a whole new big world surrounded by others who know nothing about you and could not care less about you, yet they still judge. Teenagers wouldn't be teenagers without the capacity to judge and criticize and believe that they are better than everyone else. That is why so many "groups" and "cliques" are formed during high school. Most American children go from elementary school to middle school and then on to high school. I didn't have that option. There weren't enough pre-teens on the army base to create a middle school to prepare us for going from one class to another, having different classes with different students and teachers, and to properly acclimate us to the ways of the older kids.

Instead, we were thrown into the 16- to -18-year-old world like chum for a shark. We didn't have the time to slowly walk into the ocean like baby turtles just having hatched. It is a scary world for a 12-year-old to enter! It is even scarier when you seem to have no identity other than one that is copied from others and based on incredibly low self-worth. In elementary school I could slightly pass by the judgement of others my age to some degree because the teachers were always on my side. My grades were always perfect, and I was always the first one to volunteer to do things. Everyone secretly wanted to be the "teacher's pet". In high school, I would soon be called a "nerd". A social outcast. I think all of us 7th and 8th graders trying to fit into this new territory of the Wild West that is high school found it difficult. We were still kids but had to act more mature.

The age ratio in the classes wasn't always fair either. In my Italian language class of about 25, I think there were 5 of us under the age of 14. The majority of the class was 16-, 17 and 18-year olds. They terrified me. I never wanted to speak in front of them and risk lowering my self-esteem even more should I say something stupid. In my head all I could hear them say was, "Look at that nerdy loser. She is fat and stupid and has no right to try and answer questions. Nobody likes a know-it-all."

This was my first encounter with kids older than me. Sure, I could deal with adults – I'd become a mini adult in the beginning of my life since I went to every social event my parents went to and I'd always try and fit in.

Teens were a different story. Most of the kids my age had older brothers and sisters who would often bring their friends over to their houses so at least they had a bit of prior knowledge into how a teenager's brain works. Believe me, there is a huge difference in the way a 13-year-old thinks and a 16-year-old, even though the difference is only three years.

It was during these pre-teen ages that I started to solidify behaviours that would soon haunt me. I isolated myself and I did as much research on how to lose weight (I even looked into going to a "fat camp"). Another thing I remember is going onto the internet to research eating disorders. I have no idea where the thought of an eating disorder came from – maybe TV?

This was when the internet first started invading households. Most of the websites were fairly simplistic compared to those of today. There was one website I found that was for pre-teens and it was basically a chat forum. I initiated a conversation to ask whether I was at a healthy weight for my height and asked ways to lose weight. I also asked for advice on eating disorders and how to become anorexic or bulimic. One girl gave a very accurate description and advice on how to make myself sick, but she also told me that I shouldn't do it. I wish I had taken her advice.

I was often asked to go to slumber parties and birthday parties, but I usually turned them down because that would mean I would have to be sociable and who knows what I may say… especially to boys. I had an irrational fear of boys/men back then that still continues a bit to this day. I made a mental note of every stupid comment I made and every person who ignored me, and it always ended up confirming my beliefs that my life doesn't matter, that I don't matter and that it is best if I stay invisible.

I think that even though kids and teens are young and naïve, we somehow understood the concept that if you don't like yourself, then why should I? I needed to punish myself just as much as I needed unlimited attention. It's hard to get both of those needs met at the same time.

I'd also like to share that it is not like I didn't try to seek help. I had a teacher who ironically would become one of my best friends (and replacement family). I started to tell her my issues at this early age, and Leanne always listened. Just as often as she listened, she also got increasingly frustrated that she was the only one hearing everything. She eventually told my mom everything that she knew was going on with me. I don't know if my mom truly understood, didn't believe her or just didn't know what to do. Therefore, nothing happened, and I continued to unload on Leanne. No doubt I was hurting her and her own life as much as I was hurting myself.

So, on my informal folder of medical history, let us jot down that at about 13 or 14 years of age, my eating issues escalated into bulimia, my self-esteem and self-worth were plummeting and I was laying the foundation for self-harm, which would seamlessly ease into being a part of my feeble personality a year later...

CHAPTER THREE

8:52am. Wednesday.

I hit my snooze button. *Why in the world did I choose to set Avicci's song, 'Wake me up' as my alarm sound? Fuckin A. It was once my theme song for my stay at Lampstead: it described my life at the moment to a T. The words actually could tell the tale of my life, but damn, why did I have to associate a great song with the worst thing in the world – waking up in the freaking morning!*

9:08am.

Only two snooze hits this morning. Good sign or bad sign? I'm not sure. It could either be that I got a restful night of sleep or that there are too many thoughts in my head to actually keep myself asleep. Whatever. I have until 10:00am to figure out how I'm feeling.

Women's group. Definitely not one of my top ten groups. It has the annoying quality of being a support group, with the added benefit of being that only women are allowed in. Joy. Yes, I am a woman, but a gathering of unstable hormonal women complaining about their relationships (let alone their own troubles) is a little too much for me at 10am.

I go anyway. I'm trying to be good and go to all of my groups. If they see me "behaving and trying", there is a greater possibility that I will be allowed outside the grounds unescorted. That means that I can actually see the "real world" and not be in this small, insulated bubble.

Sometimes I feel that others encase me in a bubble wrap that is slowly getting popped. I know that I am using this safety for protection, but who knows when all the bubbles will be popped and I have no armour. No cushioning to protect what is in the box labelled "fragile".

I love bubble wrap! I can't wait until I get something in the mail again so that I can hear that satisfying POP! Crushing them all at once is the best because you get to hear the crackle of a million tiny explosions, but oh the satisfaction when you pop them one by one... It's a tiny release of pressure for both parties – animate and inanimate. I want to be popped. I want to explode. I want someone to just shake me free or stomp the air out of me.

Bethany, you know that is not possible. No one can unwrap you or destroy you but yourself.

But I don't understand how this can be. A mummy can't unwrap itself because its hands are tied. So are mine, in a way. Hang on a sec, why am I thinking about bubble wrap and mummies again? I'm supposed to be focusing on what all the women are saying in the group. Shit. I hope no one asks me for my opinion...

"Ok, I'm aware of the time and since not all of you got a chance to share today, how about we go around in a circle and say how we are feeling at this moment?"

Oh Lotta, why must we do this? Is it because you know that I wasn't paying attention? Ok, quick! How am I feeling? Overwhelmed. Yes. That's an honest answer and it doesn't matter what else was said in the group.

"Overwhelmed."

"Can you identify why that is?"

Yup, Lotta definitely wanted to hear from me today. "No. I can't think of any specific reason. It is pretty much just everything in my life now! Sorry." *I think I am overwhelmed because I have no idea what I am still doing here. I am overwhelmed with all the pressures I feel that are coming from everyone, including myself. I am overwhelmed and exhausted by my constant struggle to live or die. I am overwhelmed with thoughts about what might happen to me tomorrow or the next day or in a week, a month, a year...*

On my way out of the room Lotta stops me and tells me that she, as well as the rest of the therapy team, are there for me if I need to talk to someone. I say thanks and walk out to the smoke pit.

Of course I want to talk to someone! I need *to talk to someone. I have so many random and demolishing thoughts running through my head that I need to say out loud. The only thing holding me back and probably holding back my recovery is that I have absolutely no idea how to put these thoughts into words. Not only do I have trouble talking about my feelings, but my thoughts come to me in fragments. It's hard to describe a fragment of a thought, especially when you don't even have the proper vocabulary to do so. It's like trying to describe the dream you had last night to someone. You can see it so vividly in your mind, but you can't always depict it properly. When you hear the words come out of your mouth, they don't have any meaning compared to what you experienced the previous night.*

11:00am.

Smoking "Garden".

"Bethany! It's official! I just spoke with my PA and my new racehorse is officially named Bethany! She is outstanding and so are you. You will have to come with me to see her race in a few months. It is such a beautiful name and I am so glad that I met you! I just wish you didn't smoke. Your skin looks horrible and no man will be with a girl with horrible skin who smokes."

Wow. That was definitely a compliment sandwich. Does he like me, or do I remind him of a horse? And wow, a huge blow for my self-esteem. Bethany, 0. Self-hatred, probably like a million points. I'm also slightly curious as to whether this horse is real despite the pictures I've seen… With this mishmash of patients here, it is always (well not always) hard to discern between a lie and truth, or whether the person actually believes what they say.

11:30am.

After such an uplifting conversation with my slightly "full of himself" fellow inpatient, I was more than ready to walk into the Pink Room for my next group, "Exploratory Art". This one I am really excited about. I think I have gotten more out of this group than any other here. My mind normally goes into automatic thinking and out of rational mode. Groups like this one bring out a side of me that I didn't know was hidden back there in my subconscious. There really isn't any thinking involved – it's more just your immediate reactions to things without judgements. Both Nicole and Grace do an amazing job at running this, and I barely ever get to see Nicole anymore, so it's always great to be with her.

This group's introduction doesn't comply with the normal introduction process in most other groups. Instead, we are given a giant piece of paper that is placed in the centre of the table, then we are given various art materials to make a quick representation of how we are feeling. A lot of people draw actual objects, such as trees, faces, mountains, etc… My introduction is normally a line or scribble with a darkish colour.

After the quick exercise, we say why we chose to create what we did. It is interesting to hear what people say because sometimes what they are actually feeling contradicts with how others view the image. My scribbles tend to give me leeway for a less precise answer to what it means, though often it is quite clear. If I draw a dark line at the bottom of the page, it's pretty obvious: I'm in a bad place. A lot of my circular chaotic scribbles resemble the overwhelming feelings, and when I choose to do lines it almost always ends up looking like a chart with highs and lows – not that that is always what I mean to do, but apparently that's how my subconscious works.

We are then given the topic we are supposed to work on. Today's topic is, "When I look in the mirror". *Fuck.* Somehow we are supposed to create either what we literally see or some kind of abstract image. It could be something completely different though, because it can be absolutely anything that pops into your head. They say a blank piece of paper can also speak volumes.

No. They cannot make this the topic for today. All I can think of are the words ugly, grotesque, embarrassing, fear, worthlessness and all sorts of other synonyms. As much as I feel them, I don't want to draw them and I certainly don't want to talk about them. I feel embarrassed to draw anything of the sort. I don't want people to judge the way I think of myself... though I'm not sure why. I don't want commiseration or objection. I just don't want to be.

I sit staring at my blank piece of paper for about five or ten minutes and I can feel the tears brimming in my eyes. My leg is shaking so badly from nerves that the table starts to shake a bit. *That's it. I can't do it. I can't face up to this task today.*

I run out of the room for a cigarette. For no real reason other than emotions, my adrenaline is high and

I feel the need to burn myself, so I quickly stub out my half-lit cigarette onto my wrist. I barely feel it, and since that isn't enough damage to do to myself, I start to contemplate actually running off the grounds and going to the shop to buy stuff. Luckily, Grace – my key worker who also leads the group – comes out after me to see what happened.

She could see that I was leading up to running out of the room long before I knew I was going to do it. She, too, like Laura, knows me incredibly well. She knows when I'm lying or if I'm in an incredibly hopeless state. When we talk I can somehow see my pain reflected in her eyes. She continually tells me over and over, that this is how I'm feeling "at the moment and it will pass" – one of her key phrases. She probably says it over and over to others, but for some reason I always believe her – I don't want to and often argue about it (I'm stubborn like that) – but I always hear the warmth and care that is exuded underneath the words. She delicately comes over to me and I cry onto her shoulder, repeating, "I can't do it – I can't do it." Body image at the moment isn't a topic I want to deal with, especially in a group where not everyone knows much of my past.

Grace is able to calm me down and asks if I would like to re-join the group, to just sit and listen to the others. Normally I would do this, but there are too many demons on my back right now. She walks me back to my room, gives me one last hug and reminds me that she is there for me. I ask for diazepam, take it and immediately fall asleep.

2:00pm.

It is a bittersweet moment: a fellow patient is leaving. John. He is being released into the big, bad, wild world. I am happy for him. It means that his doctor and the therapists think that he is "well" enough to make it on his own. Well, not completely on his own. He will still be seeing his therapist weekly, but he no longer has the bubble surrounding him with the knowledge that he isn't alone. A place without judgement. A place where you don't have to worry about "real" life. A place where there are constantly people around to talk to or to simply sit with. A place of nurturing.

Many patients are ready for this enormous step, and it is a very real possibility that many are not – many return several weeks after being let out. It's a simple truth to acknowledge, because no one ever really knows what life will throw at them. No one really knows how their illness will affect life outside of the hospital after inpatient treatment. I'd like to call it a somewhat hit or miss situation.

For this fellow patient of mine, all I can do is hope that he is able to use what he has learned in groups to his advantage and integrate better coping strategies into his life. I am reluctant to call him a friend simply because of the definition of being a friend to me. To me, a friend is someone who will be there for you no matter what. A friend can carry you. You know the deep stories of their past (which is certainly true here as we share some of our darkest secrets in groups) but you also know their favourite colour, their birthday, their last name… It is actually rare to know all of those things here. I know a lot of the horrors that have happened in John's life and the terrors that continue to run through his head. He was a friend while he was in here, but even though it sounds cruel, I have a hard time calling him a friend after he has left.

John and his fortitude and personality will forever be a memory, but I know that he, along with many others, will move on to a different stage in his life just as I continue to change day to day. Right now, he can only focus on himself. At this moment, he cannot carry me or be there for me. He needs to focus on himself and strengthen his own mind without worrying or thinking about those of us still here. Maybe someday I will meet up with him again, but I doubt it. We will stay in contact for a few months, but week by week we will talk less and less. It's always the same. I can only hope that one day my doubts will be proven wrong.

I troop down the corridor, following John with many other patients to say goodbye and wave him off. Routine. Normal. I give him a hug, and he returns my hug with an even stronger bear hug. I wave as his car rolls down the long driveway of the hospital and I don't stop waving until the car vanishes behind the bushes and trees. Tears are starting to run down my face. I can't help it. He is yet another loss in my life.

After what has happened to me today – and it isn't even 3:00pm – I may need to talk to Michael. He is the Magic Man – the Dumbledore of this hospital (otherwise known as the head of the therapy department). I know that whenever I speak with him I feel better. If he has time, he always welcomes patients to knock on his office door.

I knock and he opens it with a big smile, saying, "Bethany! How are things today?"

He and I both know without saying how I am doing. That's why he is the Magic Man. Michael can read minds, and he always knows what to say. I know that one day I will think of him as a key figure in my life – especially my life at Lampstead. His personality appeals to me. His wit and sarcasm, mixed with a seemingly endless mind filled with knowledge, always turned my tears into some kind of laughter. The best part are the compliments he gives me, because I truly believe him. Either he is an amazing liar, or he really means these things. I respect him immensely and believe that he is telling the truth. Michael needs some kind of equivalent of a Nobel Peace Prize for therapy.

3:00pm.

I walk slowly to the back garden to smoke and
dry my tears. As I'm finishing my cigarette, a new
nervous guy walks toward me. *Oh, why not...*

"Hi. I'm Bethany. Have you just come in?"

"Yes, a couple of hours ago." He mumbles his name
and I think it sounds like Aaron. "I hate it here. It's
weird. How long have you been here?"

*I shall dub this guy "the mumbler", as it is extremely hard
to hear/understand him.* "Oh, just a few weeks. Don't
worry. It gets better and you will meet people. If you
need anything, come find me." I start to leave, feeling
slightly better about myself for trying to help someone,
but I am quickly stopped in my tracks.

"Where are you from?"

Truth or no truth... "Ireland," I say, in my best Irish
accent (ask Shannon who is Irish – I *cannot* do the
accent!) as I open and walk through the door.

Hey, I have had a traumatic day. I can at least try
and have a little bit of fun!

3:30pm.

I take a much-needed nap after taking some more
diazepam. A particularly annoying nurse, who never
knows when to shut up, wakes me 30 minutes later.

"Bethany. How are you, and what are you doing?"
*Ugh! Learn some social skills! Obviously I am sleeping and
don't want to talk. I wouldn't be lying in my bed with my eyes*

closed if I wanted to talk! I don't have the energy to argue.

"Fine. Just sleeping." I turn my back to her and fall back to sleep.

6:00pm.

I don't even bother going down to the dining room. If the staff asks me if I ate, I'll say yes. I turn on the TV and watch some stupid B-rated movie and some weird game show where people have to see how much money they can shove into their clothes within five minutes before running through some sort of obstacle course. They get to keep whatever stays on their body after all the obstacles. It's slightly addictive to watch, and luckily there are many episodes in a row.

I wouldn't mind going on that show. I need some cash. Tripling my intake of cigarettes has made a major dent in my cash pile. I doubt they would take contestants from mental hospitals though. There has to be some kind of liability.

10:00pm.

Hot and cold shower. Meds. Sleep.

CHAPTER FOUR

I remember wanting to be a rebellious teen. I wanted to be rebellious and I wanted people to think that I was. I would go out of my way to announce anything that sounded "bad". I think that I tried smoking my first cigarette at 15 or 16 – and by saying that I smoked it, I really mean that I took a very quick puff from someone else's cigarette. I knew where the teenagers went to smoke at lunchtime and found an older teenager that I knew fairly well and asked to try it. I didn't really like the taste (I do remember her telling me that it was menthol and because of that it wasn't a "true" cigarette – ironically I now enjoy menthol) but it was something that I felt very proud of myself for doing. I wanted people to know I smoked (of course not the actual little amount I smoked) – I broke the law! I broke the "good girl" character that I had donned. I kept dropping casual hints around and no one seemed to either notice or care.

For some reason, I felt hurt that people weren't really listening to me. I only cut class once in my four years of high school and I didn't even go off the school grounds. I spent about an hour and a half just hanging out in the bathroom and wandering around the school's hallways. No one even questioned me as to why I was just roaming around. All the faculty who saw me that day thought that I had good reason to be out and about because why in the world would good, rule-abiding Bethany not be in class unless she had a reason? Teachers regularly sent me on missions to take notes to the office or to go get things because they all trusted me. So, I wasn't even noticed the one day that I technically skipped class to be a "baddie".

It was at this point in my life that I became an avid participator at the local community theatre, as well as regularly attending dance classes. After school on Mondays I rehearsed something with the school drama club, then went to tap class and then directly onward to the community theatre to rehearsals there. Tuesdays would be the same except replace tap with ballet, and then on Wednesdays it would be jazz dance classes. Thursdays I helped to lead the two lower levels of tap class before going to the theatre. Most nights I wouldn't get home until around ten o'clock at night. To this day, I have no idea how I got my homework done.

This routine lasted until I was 18 and graduated high school, and I felt like it was good for me. It kept me busy with things I enjoyed, but it also gave me a wonderful excuse to not eat dinner. I was always able to say I'd already eaten in-between one thing or another.

It was also through dance and the theatre that I got to know some older teenagers and became friends with them. I always felt so special to be a part of their group despite being two to three years younger. I especially admired one of them – Daniela – who quickly became my role model and idol. I wanted to be just like her. Forget about any other type of personality I obtained in the past, my goal was to be just like her. She was incredibly smart, talented, hilarious, thin and beautiful. Everyone loved her. Back then I don't think I realized how much I wanted her attention or how much I wanted to be like her, but I can definitely see it now. I have always found myself in need of a female role model (Leanne being one as well!) and she played the part for me at that particular time in my life.

Looking back, I can think of so many women I have put on a pedestal and worshiped in some kind of way (that sounds a bit creepy, I know!). I would do whatever they wanted in order to get their attention or to make them happy. I'm hoping it was all the work of my subconscious. So why didn't I choose to make my mom my role model? I think that part of it is the normal teenage pattern of distancing yourself from your parents, but also, I was never reprimanded for anything or ever called back to the house for "family time". It never seemed like there were any rules I had to follow. I don't know if that is the correct way of saying it, but I don't think that either my parents or I tried hard enough to keep the bond strong enough between us. I went my own way and they silently went their own, never telling me that they would have liked me to stay in the house a little bit more. We, as a family, were never good at expressing emotions, so a lot wasn't said. This was detrimental to all three of us.

The summer leading up to my senior year of high school, my mom and I took a trip around the eastern part of the United States in a search for the perfect university for me. I'd like to believe that we actually bonded for the first time. Our trip was full of laughs and new discoveries, one of which came when we went into New York City. I somewhat started to believe that I was pretty.

Now don't start thinking that my brain turned itself around all of a sudden, because it definitely didn't! I didn't think I was attractive or worthy of anything because of what I felt inside, but instead it was what was happening on the outside. In this case, words were extremely powerful. While wandering around the Metropolitan Museum of Art, a strange woman came up to me and gave me her business card. She told me that she was a representative of the Wilhelmina modelling agency and she thought that I had an extremely good chance of becoming a model. They were having an open call the next day, and she gave me the time and address to show up. I was completely dumbstruck. Out of the many people in the room of the whole museum, she came up to me... *Me*! And she was from a legit agency! She actually thought that I was beautiful enough to be a model. To this day I still can't believe it.

With the encouragement of my mom, I went to the open call and was prodded and measured and had many pictures taken of me. Apparently there are about four stages you have to get through before they offer to sign you as a client. 1 – being actually invited. 2 – passing the basic requirements of height, weight, appearance and, I'm assuming, first impressions. 3 – having everything measured and looked at (including teeth) and recorded. If you pass through those first three steps, the agents will pass along all of your info to some head office where step 4 takes place – the all-important phone call for an offer (of course, you have to pay them, but your name and photo will be sent out by the well-respected company to anyone needing models or extras for casting).

I surprised myself by passing the first three steps and was told to wait until two days later to hear back from the head office. They actually thought I was beautiful enough to get that far! Despite the excitement, I decided that that was enough for me though. It was a scary thought, yet my mom had been supportive. I had given them my grandmother's home phone number (since I didn't have a US phone at the time) but to be on the safe side, I made sure that we were out of the house during the time I may have or may not have been called.

I'll never know if they called, and I think that it is better that way. I think I would have been shattered to know that I didn't make the cut (which would just further my negative thoughts) or be left in a situation of wondering whether or not to take a stab at modelling, which would have meant that I would have had to move to the US for my last year of high school. I am still really glad that I chose not to know, because who knows what effect it would have had on my life now. But I am still amazed at the fact that I was actually approached in New York City by a modelling agency and passed so far through the process! It seems like something that only happens in the movies!

So, as I have already alluded to, self-harm swiftly came into my way of being. I think it may have started consciously as an attention seeking behaviour, but given my personality and the way I saw myself, I truly believe it was later driven by my subconscious as well.

It was never truly bad in those early years – mostly it was just surface scratches to my arms with pins, paperclips or thumbtacks, but it was visible enough for me and a couple of people around me to notice. I wanted to hurt myself, but I wasn't really sure how to do so. These were the early years of suicidal ideation as well. I was about 15 or 16 at the time and took five or six super strength paracetamol all at once during school. I think I was just trying to play a game with myself and see what it would do.

The answer is, nothing. Looking back now, I laugh at myself for thinking that tiny amount would do anything. I did end up telling a friend of mine who reported it, and I was sent to see the school counsellor for that as well as for my non-eating or making myself sick if I did have to eat. I just took it all as a joke though. It wasn't serious to me and obviously not serious for anyone else either really.

When I was 17 or 18, I actually contemplated a real suicide attempt. It was late at night and I had already had a few bottles of wine and collected all sorts of bottles of pills that I laid out in front of me. It was about to be "go time".

Ok, this may sound crazy. I still think it is crazy and so hard to believe, but I know for sure what I saw. A white owl flew past my window and perched across the street, looking at me. First of all, we don't have white owls in that part of Italy (that I know of) and secondly, even if we did, what are the chances of that happening right before I'm about to try and overdose? I swear that owl saved me. I was in such awe of what I was seeing that I completely forgot what I was going to do. I suddenly felt really tired and went to bed instead of following through with my plans.

Crazy, huh? One single event, or maybe even a bit of imagination which seemed so real, changed my future.

8:52am. Thursday.
Avicii wakes me up.

What group do I have today? I don't think I have any group that I really need to go to. I think I'll just go back to sleep. I really should go to the Self-harm group – Lori is there leading it, and I love her and hearing her opinions, but you know… Sleep is good… Yes, sleep…

12:30pm.
Despite being woken up several times by the nursing staff coming to check on me, I feel much more rested than I did hours ago. I know that I will get some kind of minor reprimand for sleeping away half the day, but ah well. What are they seriously going to do? I'm mentally ill, right?

I throw open the curtains and see that it is an incredibly gloomy looking day outside. *I should have slept longer.* It's ok though. I'm in a slightly better mood than I was in last night.

I wander out of my room to see what's happening. This is one of the most intriguing parts of the day. The first wandering out of the room to see if there is any new gossip or new patients and, most importantly, to see which staff is working the day shift. Sometimes the staff can make or break your day depending on the kind of mood you are in. I am lucky enough to see that two of the staff members I trust are working.

I cheerfully greet them, and the first words out of Lily's mouth are, "What have you been doing today?"

Ha ha. Funny one, Lily. You know I've been sleeping.

Michelle follows up with the next question of the day. "Have you had lunch yet?"

Another question that we all know the answer to.

I can see the glint in their eyes though. Even though they have extremely demanding jobs (12-hour shifts, to be precise), they always have enough energy in them to care, listen and make jokes with me. I give them one of my half smiles and announce that I have been sleeping, but it would have been more restful if they had been a bit quieter doing their checks on me and of course I haven't had lunch yet! It's only 12:30! Why on earth would I go down to eat so early? But yes, yes, of *course* I will be eating.

Yet again, all of us know that there is a 50/50 chance of it actually happening. I somewhat skip down the steps and outside to have a smoke before I do some more reconnaissance for the day.

1:00pm.
Edwina. Oh, Edwina. I can hear her high-pitched throaty cries all the way from the smoking area.

"Dr Bradley! I hate him! Look at what he has done to me! He's the crazy one! He should be locked up in here! He never listens to a thing I say and he better be careful because I have figured out some secrets of his! He takes his bicycle out at lunchtime and meets with his mistress! What a fool! A fool, I tell you! I shall write to the papers about this."

I saunter into the downstairs lounge as she continues with her rant. She is still wearing her teal blue robe, that I assume was at one point super comfy, and her slightly see-through and tea-stained white dressing gown. Despite her ragged appearance, messy grey hair and the slightly crazed look in her eyes, I have a great fondness for her. She has won me over and, apparently, she feels the same toward me. When she feels agitated she often seeks me out, and I quite willingly sit with her.

One personal satisfaction I get from her is knowing that she has been living here at Lampstead for over ten years. There is no way that will be happening to me! Her stories and disturbances are almost always the same – they're usually about her consultant, Dr Bradley, the nursing staff or her friends that are constantly doing something to upset her. And being the proper Englishwoman as she claims to be, she despises Kate Middleton (Prince William's wife) as well as the former Prime Minister of the UK, Margaret Thatcher. Once she gets a rant going on any one of these topics, it is extremely hard to calm her down unless you know her well enough, which I like to think I do; the staff often end up making her more enraged.

The thing with Edwina is that she may be in the later years of her life and is still very intelligent, but she also seems to have the mind of a six-year-old. All she needs is a simple distraction. Anything will do really: flowers, pictures, music… What I find works especially well is talking about her favourite book, *Jane Eyre*. This happens to be one of my favourite books as well, and since she found out about that I have been invited to her room for tea and readings of *Jane Eyre*. We swoon over Mr Rochester and visualize the wildness of the moors. I think both of us have a bit of the Jane Eyre personality in us that attracts us to this particular piece of literature.

If the book isn't a good enough distraction for the traumas going on in her head, I also have one back-up prepared. We discuss Julius, her stuffed elephant. Even after all this time, I am still not sure if she believes he is real or if she is "with it enough" to realize that he is just a stuffed animal. Either way, it doesn't matter. Julius is her child; she dotes on him like he is alive. I suppose if you have been living here in the hospital for this long, you would want a constant companion such as Julius.

Note to self: start carrying around Safari, my stuffed lion, and begin to have conversations with him… possible coping strategy or at least a means of entertainment.

Side note: at one point during my stay at Lampstead, I "adopted" a coconut named Wilber from the dining room, as well as a pineapple, and carried them around with me just to see what people would say.

According to Edwina, Julius calls me Auntie Bethany. I feel privileged to be a part of his life. I have heard and witnessed other patients wanting to hold Julius or simply ignore him. If this happens, Edwina will most definitely chastise them. If you greet Edwina, you must greet Julius. Whenever I go into Edwina's room for one of our readings, I always bring a little something for her and for Julius. If Julius doesn't like you then neither does Edwina, so I'm glad that he chooses to like me! In fact, I am one of the very few people who have been allowed to hold Julius and to "babysit" him while she visits the therapy department. And because I am his auntie, I get the updates on how well he is doing on his studies.

Apparently his reading is coming along wonderfully and he loves to read Dr Seuss, but he completely fails in the math department just like his mom and aunt. What a shame.

I am able to comfort Edwina quite quickly this time by complimenting Julius on how stately he looks today. I offer her a tea, which she readily says yes to (I knew she would), and we start to discuss many extremely random topics, such as the time she fell in love with a man and about their trek up a hill on ponies for a picnic on the top. By the time our conversation was over, she was ready for a nap and I had to figure out what to do with the rest of my day.

3:00pm.
I have a few cigarettes and walk back into the room to watch some more of *Friends*. I can say all of the lines without even watching the screen, and since I know what will happen I can feel my eyes start to droop slightly. Before I can do anything about it, I am fast asleep.

6:00pm.
Some kind of clumpy stew thing is on the menu, so I opt for some bread and cheese. Another cigarette and I'm back up to my room.

I have realized that cigarettes are like currency here. The more you have, the more people gather around you and beg (and obviously like you!). I believe I am a charitable person, but there comes a limit and if you are constantly asking for one, I will most likely cut you out of the receiving end.

There are people I know who will return the favour if I forget my ciggys upstairs, and those who I know will give me a new pack in the same situation once they are able to get to the shop. I am not worried about them. There are also the charity cases – the people who just arrived and the caring ones who seriously don't have any money. Everyone else gets one or two chances to see what kind of a person they are, and just like Santa Claus, I put a check mark next to their name as to whether they are good or bad (at repaying the cigarette to me or others).

6:45pm.
I turn the TV on and flip through the channels until I get to the two movie channels. *Great – they are playing the movie* Rio *yet again. Every night for the past week? Some kind of conspiracy.* I watch it anyway, and before I know it, it is meds time once again. I line up behind all those eager patients waiting to get their drugs that will transport them to a world outside this hospital. It's the best part of the day, many people say. I quickly swallow mine, take a shower, watch a bit of *Family Guy* and fall asleep. It feels like it's been a long day, but nothing really happened... Sleep.

"To sleep, perchance to dream..." (Hamlet, Act III, Scene 1).

CHAPTER FIVE

Communication. It is one word and yet the meaning and immensity is often lost to most. We are born with the knowledge of how to communicate – a baby cries when its needs aren't being met or smiles when it is happy – but for some reason, the ability to communicate is lost to many of us as we grow older. I'm not sure of the exact age that I lost the ability to effectively communicate, but I know for sure that I lost it sometime during my teenage years.

On a conscious level, I partially stopped communicating for fear of ridicule, but there must also have been a part of me that unconsciously lost the ability. I lost the words to explain my needs, explain my hopes, explain my sadness and anger. I lost communication with myself. I became what other people needed me to be, and in turn, I became their reflection. I figured that if I couldn't communicate with myself, maybe being on the same wavelength as another would be better. It would be a better version of myself because obviously those around me knew who they were and could state what they wanted to themselves as well as to others. The problem with communication is that it is a two-way street. Remember that – it is a very important point.

By the time I turned 18, any sense of myself had absolutely disappeared, or maybe it had become so entwined in the mass of scars and personas that were a part of my body that I didn't know what was what.

I had done an amazing job at keeping potential long-lasting friendships at bay. The only people who were actually a part of my life as I left Italy and ventured to the US for university were my parents, my dog Sandy, and Leanne and her husband Paul. At that point in time, getting on that plane and heading to a new world was one of the most terrifying and unsettling events of my life. Forget any issues I had with eating, self-harm or depression – this experience topped the cake for me. Saying goodbye to the only world I had known and to the only people left in that world for me turned me inside out. Tears poured out of me from the night before I left for the airport until about four months into my first year of uni – and this was only because it was December and I was going to be returning to Italy for Christmas.

I'm sure that I was a pleasure to sit next to on all of my flights as I tried to silently cry in-between sips of the lovely alcohol provided for free on transatlantic flights. Little did those passengers know that they were sitting next to a future inpatient at a psychiatric hospital!

For most teenagers going to college is about escaping home and having freedom for the first time. For me, it was about trying not to panic about not being at home and wondering what to do with my new-found freedom. I didn't really like the thought of freedom being in a completely new environment. I wanted familiarity, and there was nothing familiar about this country that I found myself in, nor was there familiarity in my nationality.

So there I was in the grand ol' US of A and I felt like such a foreigner even though I was in my own country. It felt like complete dissociation. I didn't feel comfortable in Italy, despite being born there, but on the other hand, I felt like a total imposter living in the US.

One simple example that continued to perplex me was the act of tipping. In Italy, you never tip for anything. In the States, not only do you have to tip practically everyone, but you also have to know what the appropriate percentage is to tip. This completely threw me. From the get-go I was lost. I landed in the US and got a taxi to the hotel I was staying in until I was allowed into the dorms. At the end of the 45-minute journey, I knew the total amount of the fare and yet I had no idea how much to tip the driver or if it was perhaps included. Talk about landing wheels up.

This and many other seemingly common sense actions were completely unknown to me. Whenever I

asked those around me what to do (such as where do I
go to mail a package or even how to order a coffee at
a Starbucks), people would look at me and stare. "But
you are American!" they'd say, as well as, "What do
you mean when you say that you don't know whether
or not to seat yourself at a table in the restaurant?"
Or even better, "Duh, of course when you order food
delivery it comes straight to you – yes, of course they
will call and tell you when they are there!" I appeared
to them to be a lunatic before I was actually diagnosed
with a mental illness.

It was also at this point in my life that I started
hating the question, *Where are you from?* Even the people
in the US didn't understand my story. "Wait. So you
are obviously American, but you grew up in Italy?
That is so weird! Shouldn't you have an accent of
some sort? I had a cousin go to Rome for Christmas
once. Did you meet him?"

Oh. My. God. It seemed as if everyone I met had
never left the country, let alone the state, and they
couldn't believe there were other places in the world
worth visiting. Here I was at only 18 and had not only
seen almost all of Italy *(no, I did not meet your cousin –
Rome is a huge ass city!)*, but I had visited almost every
single European country and many, many US states.

However, many things greatly excited me. I could
go shopping in malls with so many stores! I could
have almost any kind of food I wanted! I could go to a

movie theatre that had more than one screen or have a TV with more than five channels! Overall though, I was more like a kid in Disney World. The novelty and excitement wears off, and you wonder, "When am I going to go home and have to stop worrying about what is around the next bend?"

I had to deal with all sorts of other practical issues as well. Try getting a driver's license in the States without actually having a home residency address in an actual state, or for that matter, even applying to vote and figuring out which state you belong to. The university I went to was a fairly small liberal arts school and most of the students (probably about 97% of them) lived within a few hour's drive or even a short plane ride away from home. This wasn't the case for maybe the other 3% of them, but they had other relatives or close family friends in the area.

The only reason I mention this here is because the university completely shut down over the Easter break, Thanksgiving break and Christmas to save on the cost of electricity, heating and staff. This was always ok for me at Christmas because I could definitely go home for the four weeks we were given, but it wasn't as practical (or cost effective) to fly for ten hours to Italy every time we were given a three or seven daybreak.

Students were not allowed to stay on campus during these breaks, so I found myself continually wondering where I would go for their duration. I ended up flying to my grandmother's house in Illinois for Thanksgiving twice (despite the fact that I didn't know her too well). Other breaks I spent at hotels, at a few of my university friends' houses and for a couple of Spring Breaks, my parents paid for me to fly back to Italy because I was so incredibly homesick (I think I may now be able to label it as depression). I once spent "Turkey Day" (Thanksgiving) at my friend Clara's house in Florida. Clara and I first met in first grade back in Italy, and through the years we had managed to keep in touch and remain friends. To this day we continue to talk – albeit not for many months at times, but we can somehow catch up from when we last talked. She is probably the only person I have known my entire life and I am still not sure how that happened.

So yes, all of these issues were enough stress for a normal person to have to deal with, but add on my ever-increasing depression, eating disorders and self-harm and we have a winning combination for an accident waiting to happen.

8:52am. Friday.
Same routine – Avicii, snooze, meds, snooze, snooze, yawn, wander into the pre-lit bathroom, Red Bull, check staff, check for newbies, smoke, answer stupid questions, group.

10:00am

Upper Court support group. At least Tori is leading the group. She always seems to calm me and always makes me laugh and feel comfortable. She is the one who taught me to knit and make origami among many other things. She is my age, and I wish she could be my friend in real life – not just in Lampstead life. No matter how much I love her and admire her, today is a really low day for me, and all I can express to the group is my name and the fact that I am feeling really low. I am surrounded by others and yet I feel completely alone.

  Just like a tsunami, it hits me, and just like a tsunami, I can see it coming. I see the tide recede and wait for the wave to hit. It's hard to breathe. My leg starts to shake. *What are they saying? Did someone say my name? If they did, I don't care.* I am in my own world now. I am drowning in my own thoughts. *How is that possible? Are my thoughts so deep and vast that it is possible to actually sink? Breathe in and breathe out. Breathe in and breathe out. Oh God, what am I doing here? Why am I alive? I can't do this. What's the point in all of this? There is nothing I have hope for. There is no one who cares enough about me. Sure, my parents love me. Sure, I know that there are staff here who care, but do they really care or are they just acting because it is their job to do so? There are some friends in different places around the world, but there is no one actually* here. *Next to me or in my head. I am alone and there's nothing to look forward to. Absolutely nothing. What is the difference between a long shitty life or a short shitty life if it is just shit to begin and end with? Why not just end the suffering for myself as well as those who have to deal with me? It would be so easy... Bethany!*

Ok, I'm in the room again. I'm still breathing and I'm still shaking. My body aches and so does my heart. I never understood heartbreak until now. My heart is breaking for itself. I feel tears in my eyes but luckily they don't drop. I don't want it to happen here. Or maybe I do. I know Tori would definitely help me. She would let me cry and I would feel the emotion emanating from her. Or if not Tori, I want to cry in someone's embrace or cry in front of Laura, Shannon, Lotta, Grace, Julia, Megs, Lily, Michael... practically any one of the therapists or staff. *Hold me. Keep me alive. Don't let me go.*

Group is over and I slowly walk out to a different smoking area where I know I won't be bothered. I am trembling. I try and sit it out, but I can't stop shaking. This isn't going to work.

Instead, I walk around the grounds of the hospital and try to be "mindful" about what I'm seeing. I see a squirrel running through the trees. I see a few flower buds starting to bloom. I hear a kid screaming in the adolescent unit. *I shudder internally.* I see a cloud above me. It looks like a turtle. I smile a bit. I see one of the patients playing with a dog on the lawn. My smile gets a lot bigger.

Then I see a sharp piece of glass in the gravel. My mindful walk is over. My demons start to return. *Not yet. Please stay away for the moment. I really want to go to my next group, and I want to still cry. Breathe in. Breathe out. Just breathe.*

11:30am.
I made it. I sit on the carpeted floor in what was once the chapel of this old building. The stained-glass windows still filter the light into the room and the walls still allow a deep echo. I can feel the history here. I can feel the presence of previous patients in the room. There is something soothing about this feeling. I think about all the stories these ornate walls must have heard over their hundreds of years. How many cries? How many laughs? How many broken souls?

Many people think that psychiatric hospitals are creepy, and I can agree to a certain extent. But when most people think of mental hospitals, they think of the old type of asylums with people in straitjackets and places where lobotomies regularly take place. It's not like that. Well, at least it isn't like that at Lampstead. I actually don't doubt that this place has its scary ghosts, but there is something somewhat serene rather than eerie about the air here. The ghosts that may be here are calming ghosts trying to understand and help those still living in this difficult world and in these challenging minds. Every now and again you feel some kind of calming presence surrounding you and before you know it, it is gone. I understand this place and its history. I understand the solace that this building has provided for people, as well as the fear that it has instilled. I am a part of Lampstead just as much as it is a part of me.

My reverie is broken as other people start to file into the room for the Creative Writing group. It is ok, though: I have spent too much time in my head already. I need to interact. I need to embrace these people around me instead of holding them away. I need to feel them surrounding me so I don't feel so alone and worthless in this world.

I fill in the sign-in sheet once it reaches me.

Name: Bethany Hacker
Consultant: Dr Ramsey
Ward: Upper Court

Ok. I'm here – physically and mentally.

This mid-morning group – creative writing – is one of my favourites and I hate that I have to wait until Fridays to attend it. I want it to be on every day. *Well, I guess I want all of my favourite groups to be every day. They should really create a schedule based on my likes. I've been here long enough! Hmm… if I ever get out of here, maybe I can get them to name something after me. Maybe a room or a bench?*

Oh, the outdoor smoking gazebo would be good, or maybe a whole wing of the hospital! My insurance has definitely kept this place in business!

Creative writing is not only good because it is a creative group, but I also love the therapist and therapy assistant who run it, Megs and Safiya. They make a great team. I assume they have been running this group together for a long time since they tend to finish each other's sentences.

This group always starts out with a mini "warm up" where, of course, we say our names and how we are feeling, but we are also asked to answer a question posed to us by the therapists. Today we have to think about what three items we would take with us if we had to be stranded on a deserted island.

What?! Only three things? If we knew we were going to be stranded, why couldn't we pack a suitcase or a whole boatload of crates? Ok. I need to be practical about this. I need to pick two necessary items and then something that I just like. Wow, I am taking this seriously for a fun activity. But who knows, maybe someday I'll actually be in this situation!

I listen as the group goes around and I hear things like guns, knives, water or a water purifying system, iPods, toilet paper, laptops, phones, a friend and on and on and on…

I thought that I was taking this too seriously but nope! A water purifying system? Seriously?! And what are you going to do with your electronics once the battery runs low? No place to

charge them! Ha! I got you! You have no power source, silly!
Awesome. I'm going near last. I can be as creative, funny or
practical as I want.

"Hi, I'm Bethany and I'm not doing very well this
morning. I almost didn't make it here but I'm glad
I did. I think the three things I'd bring to the island
would be a really long book that has a pencil attached
to it somehow so I can write in the margins, the
biggest bottle of vodka ever produced for drinking
and maybe sterilization if anything is left, and then a
stuffed animal for company. *So yes, practical and fun.*

Safiya then leads the group in a mindfulness exercise
to get us ready to write. We are told to get into a
comfortable position, close our eyes and focus on our
breathing. In for six counts and then out for four. When
breathing out, it should be as if we are breathing out
through a straw, forcing a noise to be made.

This always bothers me. I don't want anyone to
hear me breathing. Oh well, I go with it. I wonder if
others have this same fear, because I don't hear too
much sound as we are supposed to be breathing out.

Safiya has the perfect voice to lead us through these
mindfulness exercises. She keeps a calm steady tone
as she has us imagining we are walking along a beach,
taking a boat across the water and onto a jungle island.
Through this imagery we are guided past beautiful
creatures and waterfalls and eventually back to the boat
to take us back to the main sandy island. It is at this point,

once we are relaxed and our outside worries are left behind, that the topic of today's writing is announced: if we were given a chance to change one thing from our past, what would it be? The whole group groans. This will not be an easy subject and we all know it.

The therapists tell us in the beginning that this isn't an actual writing class and there is no need to worry about grammar or what it sounds like, and we can go into the topic as deep or as surface level as we want to. Of course, me being me, I want it to be perfect. So what would I change?

I honestly can't think of anything. Actually, I know what I would change – the whole fact that I am actually alive at this moment. I would change every single choice that I made in the past – not just one thing. So either I would be a completely different person or not alive at all. At least then I wouldn't be sitting here and pondering over my failures in life and hopelessness for the future…

My piece of paper remains blank. There is nothing for me to say that wouldn't worry the therapists and completely ruin my chances of ever getting out again. Not only that, but my thoughts are so far away I don't even know where to start writing. It's better to have a blank page than have a bunch of jibber-jabber, right? Oh well.

I feel so guilty – like I've let down Megs and Safiya. I know it is supposed to be about me, but I feel like I should have been able to complete the "assignment".

Now I feel even worse about myself.

We are split up into groups of two or three and we read aloud to our group what we have written. My partner is lucky. Or am I the lucky one? She doesn't seem to care that I didn't write anything because she spends the whole time reading hers and talking about it. I don't think that I even needed to be sitting there. It made it easier on me though. I could just listen and tell her how good her paper was without having to give much input or thought to the matter.

Once finished, Megs asks us to come back to the circle again where we are given time to share our thoughts to the group as a whole. Yet again, I can feel the eyes of Megs and Safiya looking at me, wondering about what I'm thinking. Yet another case of "don't make eye contact, Beth!"

The whole no eye contact thing is hard for me – I hate not looking at people when they are talking. Nevertheless, I manage to get through the session without having to share much; but yet again, I know that they sensed my low mood.

As I walk out of the door, Megs winks at me and says, "Don't you worry Bethany. It will come. You just have to keep fighting – and don't forget, I believe in you!" I give her one of my half smiles and say thanks, trying hard not to let the tears flow down my face. *So many people seem to care about me. Why won't I allow them to and why can't I appreciate it?*

1:10pm.

I choose not to go for a smoke. I think that I've been smoking a bit too much recently and it is taking its toll on my throat as well as my bank account.

Instead, I actually force myself to walk into the dining room. I've spent the day wallowing and I need to nourish myself both mentally and physically. The menu looks pretty much the same as it always does except there is the option for soup. *Don't people get tired of getting full meals three times a day?*

I'm lucky, though. It's a good soup today – lentil. The kitchen staff are slightly surprised to see me there for lunch as I ask for the soup and some bread. I find an empty table and sit down, then take my phone out of my pocket to play with and pretend to be busy. *What did people do before there were phones to keep up the illusion of being busy and having something to do?* Nowadays it seems as though everyone has a phone in their hands whilst waiting for something. Heaven forbid we look awkward and appear to have nothing to do with our hands while waiting. Think about it, if you see someone standing outside a door to a store or sitting somewhere just looking around, aren't you just a bit suspicious? The immediate thought is that there is something wrong with the picture you are seeing. Something must be wrong. Actually engaging with the world is uncommon these days it seems.

My soup is actually delicious and I'm proud of myself for eating. Crazy, eh?

2:00pm.

Friday afternoons are normally my "free" times. This doesn't necessarily mean that I don't have anything to do, it just means that I have no groups that are recommended for me to go to. I spend most Friday afternoons seeing all the people on my "support" team.

First is normally Grace, my key worker. Her job is to sort out my group schedule and make sure everything is working out for me, but I think that the fact that I have been here for 50 million years lets her off the hook on that one. The schedule she wrote up for me many months ago is fairly useless. At this point in time I know exactly what groups are taking place and when. It is now pretty much up to me to decide whether or not to go to them – though she does still push for me to go to a few groups that I dislike (Coping Strategies and Movement).

Instead, I use the time I have with her to discuss things that have happened during the week and how I am feeling – a mini therapy session. I have known Grace for a little more than two years now, and I think I know pretty much everything she is going to say. One of her most common phrases is "that's how you are feeling now," and the occasional "yet that will change". I can pretty much have the entire conversation while she sits quietly next to me as I speak both sides. Nevertheless, she has become a source of comfort in my life. I thoroughly enjoy her company.

A few of the best experiences I had here were when she put time aside during her work day to take me outside of the Lampstead grounds. I wasn't (and still am not) allowed to leave without an escort, but she made it possible to take me to several gorgeous parks and to quaint little towns so that I could start adapting to life outside of the Lampstead bubble. My favourite day was when we just sat by a river. I never knew how much water calmed me until that day.

Today's talk is much the same as it always is: I tell her about my depressive episodes and disassociation and everything that feels wrong in my life (it feels like the list is never ending sometimes). As expected, she tells me that is how it feels at the moment and things will get better. She believes in me.

I hate that people have so much faith in me and believe in me so much. I'm afraid that if I screw up somehow that they will never trust me again... I try and make a few jokes to try and lighten the situation. Somehow, I always manage to make her laugh which makes me feel quite good about myself... *Maybe I should become a comedian.*

Before she leaves I tell her about one of my strange dreams, about how a peacock was chasing me down a seemingly never-ending spiral staircase and I just couldn't get away. It was horrifying, especially because I could see my cat on the ground and I just wanted to get to her before something bad happened!

Of course Grace laughed, but I'm still left with that dream and questioning why I was so scared of a spiral staircase with a peacock chasing me. Oh well.

She asks me if I've been eating. "Let's play a little game. You get to decide whether I have eaten full meals or if I have eaten nothing or just little snacks sporadically." I grin. *It is against my nature to lie but I don't want to tell the truth outright – I'll get in trouble!*

"Bethany, we know each other well enough and we both know the answer to that question."

"Ok. Fine. No, I have barely eaten in the past few days." I'm looking down and trying not to blush for being called out so quickly. *Why do I have such a strong conscience? Without one it would be so easy to lie!* I look back up at her and see her concern.

I hate that I bother people so much. Why can't I get my shit together?

"Bethany, you just have to do it. I'm not asking for much. Just a little bit at meals. The lack of nutrition in your body only brings you deeper into depression. You know that. And what about self-harm and your suicidal thoughts?"

Again, I find myself looking down and realize I haven't said anything in response. *Can I lie through this one too? Ugh! No.* "I haven't done anything yet, but yes, suicide is a constant thought and… yeah…"

I take a long pause and wonder whether to continue or not. Sometimes she starts to talk again and doesn't let me have the long pause, but not this time. Silence. *Shit. I hate the silence. Here I go...*

"Well, um, I have been thinking of hurting myself pretty badly. But I haven't done anything yet!" I quickly add... but the 'yet' catches her attention – damn words.

"Do you have anything in your room?"

Now what? Outright admit it, and Grace will turn it in to the staff. Say no, and she will tell the staff anyway and they will search my room. There is the possibility that they won't find anything... No, I respect Grace too much. "Yes. I have shards of glass and razor blades, as well as a CD that I broke into sharp pieces."

"Where?"

I walk slowly over to my tissue box and take the blades out from under the tissues, then walk into the bathroom and shake out the glass and shards from my box of tampons.

"Thank you, Bethany. I'm proud of you. Is there anything else?"

I shake my head and try to conceal the tears running down my face. *Do I have anything else? I honestly don't remember. I've hidden things in so many random places that I can't really remember anymore. But I can honestly say no because I can't think of what or where!*

She gives me a comforting hug. I really love hugs so much. So many emotions can be conveyed in a hug. Being here at Lampstead has given me the good fortune of having many hugs. I have come to realize that it is also quite awkward to hug someone when you are much taller than the other person. I'm 5'10", which is quite tall for a girl, so it is a bit awkward to hug guys who are shorter (as well as other females, I guess). Where do you put your arms? Do you give the hug where both arms are over the shoulder or both arms around the chest? Another option is the one arm around the shoulder and the other around the chest. Like I said: awkward, especially if you are the one who initiates the hug. One of the most hilarious continuations of hugs I've had here is with this extremely short man. He *loved* hugs and I now realize why. When he hugged me, his head came right under my breast. So not only did he get the warmth of the hug, but also a bit of inappropriate touching.

Grace told the staff about the items in my room after she turned them in to them and they did a cursory room search, which involved me standing by my door while they tried to go through everything in my room. It's nearly impossible to find anything in here. I have accumulated too much crap in the many months here. The staff just have to take my word that I have nothing else, though they are aware that if I want to cut myself, I can find almost anything to do the job. Even easier, I can just continue to burn my skin with my cigarette!

3:30pm.

I decide to go outside to the smoking garden for a cigarette and see a few of my friends playing ping-pong (we may be mental and in a nuthouse, but we can still have fun!). I take a turn and fail miserably. I forget how much hand eye coordination you need for even the simplest of sports. I laugh it off because I can only imagine what I look like.

4:00pm.

Yay! I get to see Laura again. Is that sarcasm? I actually don't know, which is a tad scary. The session goes almost exactly the same as last time. We have basically the same conversation that I just had with Grace, except Laura is a bit more on the stern side.

I get slightly distracted throughout the session as I hear people outside laughing and still playing ping-pong. It's quite weird. Talking about your deepest fears and thoughts and saying you want to hurt yourself when you are listening to such joyous laughter outside. It's surreal.

The session ends in a non-dramatic way and I casually walk back to my room to grab another Diet Coke and let the nursing staff know that I am back from my therapy session, and that I'm off to see my psychiatrist, Dr Ramsey.

5:15pm.

I take a seat in one of the very posh chairs in the waiting room until she calls me into her office. The magazines on the table are what you would expect to see in a psychiatrist's waiting room: *Town and Country*, *City Life*. Something about gardening and wildlife… In other words, soothing magazines. I'm glad I chose a comfy seat because the waiting room starts to fill up with other patients for other psychiatrists who share the office space. A few stand awkwardly by the water machine. I'm about ready to give my seat away to one of them, but Dr Ramsey calls me in before I can make the kind gesture. I did my good act for the day even if it was only a thought in my head!

"Would you like to…" She never finishes the sentence because I am already up and out of my seat, practically in the office already. "There we are," she says, pointing at my seat as she sits herself down as well.

She is a wonderful consultant, but I always laugh at this beginning of our meetings. Of course I would like to come in and sit down. That is why I am here after all!

"Let me just find your notes here. I know my secretary left them for me. Here we are. I tried to look up what the staff have written about your week on the computer, but the system isn't working again so I apologize for that."

For all the money that goes into this hospital, one would like to think the little things like patients' care notes would be accessible by computer when necessary!

"So, tell me, how are you doing?"

I know I needn't go into great detail with Dr Ramsey. First of all, she can read me like a book and I know she can tell just from the shaking of my leg that I'm not doing too well, but I still give her the nutshell summary and then answer that I still have no idea what will be happening with me in the future. I have no real plans other than possibly going back to university to get my master's degree if and when I ever get out of here.

"Any trouble with any of your meds?"

"No, but would it be possible to up them a little bit? I've been on the same dosage for a long time and still feel extremely depressed."

"I don't think so, Bethany. For you, I think what will benefit you most will be the therapy, not the medication."

Fine. I tried, and she is probably right. She walks me to the door and tells me to just keep going and take it easy this weekend. *Yeah, like there is anything to do other than take it easy. Ping-pong is probably the most stressful thing I will be doing.* I thank her and wander back to the ward.

6:00pm.

I decide to take a quick nap to avoid making the
choice of dinner and because I am so damn tired.
I blame the ping-pong.

8:00pm.

The night staff wake me up as they parade into my
room doing their "Good Evening" routine. I can't
believe no one woke me up sooner. At least there is
still some hope that I will sleep tonight. The night is
still young, after all, and the nights can be the most
"fun". And yes, those air quotes are for sarcasm. We
do have fun, just the kind of fun you had when you
were ten years old on a Friday night. Not the kind
of fun that I would like to be having right now, such
as going to a movie and then a bar afterward to get
pretty drunk.

I am not disappointed as I walk into the lounge
area. Someone has put on some action DVD and
others have already started to play Monopoly. We
pass the night eating junk food (yes, even I have a few
crisps), playing games, watching TV, and smoking and
joking. There is a good crowd of people in here at
the moment, and they all have a wonderful sense of
humour and a desire to do something other than sit
in their rooms.

It's a good thing that the therapists don't hear
some of the stuff we talk about because then we

would probably all be locked up forever. We can be quite crude.

All of our sleeping meds finally kick in at about midnight, though we try to fight against them. It's a losing battle. The drugs always win. One by one the patients try and carry themselves back to their rooms. We finish the game of Sorry! that seems to go on forever (I won! Oh yeah!) and I'm left in the room by myself. My old housekeeper habits come over me and I clean the room up a bit before stumbling back to my room. I quickly brush my teeth, take out my contacts and immediately fall into a dreamless sleep.

CHAPTER SIX

Have you ever felt completely alone, or had the sense that you are in a constant dream world and everything around you is just happening and you are a silent witness? It's this dreamlike state that is disorientating. You dissociate with yourself and the world around you. It's terrifying to think about, but when you are in that state you don't even feel the terror. You just feel numb. Well, that's what I am feeling now and that's how I was beginning to feel during my four years at college.

I had very few friends (well, close friends) throughout my years at university. I always felt out of place and, of course, I was. I had no idea where my place was. In my first year I thought I was starting to become a real "American". I enjoyed my first Halloween hayride, sledding down hills on our dinner trays in the snow, went to my first diner (at 3am – craziness!), went to a real mall on my own, went on my first date, stayed up for an all-nighter and went to a few parties.

I also got to experience having a roommate for the first time. I did not enjoy that. I'm an only child, remember. I don't share and I like my own space. I felt like a real adult for the first time in my life. In Italy, life is pretty much dependent on your parents or those older than you. American teens can't drive in Italy, nor can they really go out anywhere together or do anything without an adult being around. Well, I'm not sure if that is a generalization of teens in Italy or just my experience!

I was so excited that at the age of 18 and 19 I could ride around in my friends' cars and just go out somewhere on a whim. One exciting day we just went to the grocery store to get burgers and stuff to create an unplanned BBQ. The day my friends drove me down to the New Jersey shore was one of the most memorable experiences for me because it was just so unheard of for me to do. Anyone reading this who grew up in the US is probably rolling their eyes right now about how stupid all this seems, but for me, every day was a new adventure.

Looking back, I think too many new things were happening to me too quickly. Moving to a new country, meeting new people, learning how to live like a teen, learning how to live like an American, and I also have to add in that little bit called going to university classes.

As mentioned previously, I never really had trouble with school. Throughout college I was pretty much able to slide by without working much and I was still able to get good grades. Life may have turned out differently for me had I actually dedicated myself to a specific subject and immersed myself in that world. Being decent at most subjects (I'm specifically avoiding my absolute ghastly knowledge in math) made it difficult for me to choose a major. I went from being a Theatre major to a Biology major, then Spanish and Anthropology, and finally settled on a Political Science major and Latin American studies minor, mostly because I had the most class credits in those fields. Luckily, I at least enjoyed those subjects and spoke some Spanish.

Throughout the four years I slowly became more and more depressed and started drinking more. The few friends I had started to disappear from my life as I isolated myself and drank. My eating behaviours became stranger and stranger. I'd go weeks without eating and only drinking, then a week or two of ordering delivery for like three people and eating most of it, then making myself sick. Every once in a while I ate "normal" meals (I actually have no idea if they were normal as I still have no idea what a normal meal is) with everyone else in the cafeteria.

One of my regrets that I still have is the fact that all of the pictures from my university graduation show my bloated face from my massive drinking binge (yet restricting food) in the final week. I still cringe at the pictures. I wish I could look at the pictures and see the fun times and show a person much proud of herself and proud of all that she accomplished. I also wish I had taken more pictures of me with my parents on graduation day, but I was too embarrassed to take so many when I knew I looked awful.

One wonderful thing introduced to me during those college years was the ability to seek help from professionals at the counselling centre on campus. I met with two people there who I truly believe changed my life – I didn't know it then, but I think it sunk in subconsciously. These two people helped me to realize that I actually had true problems that needed attention. I wasn't just exaggerating, and it wasn't just something I had concocted. There were people who I could talk to and who would listen to me; I was able to open up just a bit and that little bit is what I think helped me – especially in the coming years. I dare to say that they saved my life because they were several of the first people who had faith in me and who kept that spark of life in me when I thought everything was gone. They were two of the people I still miss the most from my university. They have no idea how much they helped me to survive those final years at the school.

I graduated in May 2008 and returned immediately to Italy without any direction or idea for the future. What could combine my degree in political science with a love for animals? The Humane Society

Legislative Fund in Washington DC of course. I, once again, left Italy in tears in August 2008 to become an intern. I was left facing the same issues I had when I went to college, with the added guilt that my parents were paying for a place to live and all the living costs because, of course, I was an unpaid intern!

I moved back to Italy in December of that year to a soulless job working at the hotel on the military base and became a Housekeeping Team Leader. I met many amazing people there and made a best friend – Magdala – who taught me how to make real Italian food! I love her still and we try to keep in touch.

Despite meeting so many great people (and characters), my job continued to sink my mood even lower. Back then, at least I knew that if I stayed working at that hotel, I would never get anywhere in life and I wanted to do something to change that. Wow, at that point I still had more than a glimmer of hope left in me! I realized that I have a degree, and after all of that education I'm cleaning toilets?!

But life started to unravel quicker than I could make knots to slow things down. I knew at that point that I needed help.

Saturday. 9:52am.
Yay! I get an extra hour of sleep before my day officially begins. Support group on a Saturday doesn't start until 11am, which I believe is a much

better schedule. Well, only because it means I can be extremely lazy and sleep more.

I would have thought that they'd have us on a more rigid schedule, seeing as sleeping does the body good but not always the mind. Yes, all of the disturbing thoughts disappear when you are sleeping, but that also means that you aren't dealing with them and talking them through with the professionals who are there to do their job. What it really comes down to is whether you (or your insurance) are paying for you to come to a highly rated psychiatric facility to get help because you want to get better, or if all you want is a brief vacation from real life.

To me, it doesn't really matter at this moment, so I grab a Red Bull, contemplate changing out of my PJ's, decide to, then quickly walk through the maze to the therapy room.

I thought I was late but apparently not as there are only three other people in the room, plus the therapist. *Fuck. Hang on a second, Bethany. Maybe this situation isn't going to be as bad as you think. Crap. Now I'm starting to sound like the therapists. I guess it was bound to happen at some point.*

I have my trepidations as I walk into the room. "Hi, Bethany. Do you happen to know if anyone else is coming this morning?" *Good, it's Grace working this Saturday. I can talk with her if I need to. She always makes me feel comfortable and safe. It's a weird feeling not being safe in a building that is supposed to be nurturing and supportive.*

"I have no idea. I didn't see anyone walking this way."

The group ended up being ok with just a few of us. There was a newbie in the group so she had a lot to say and many questions. In her introduction, she said that she was fine. Me, being the veteran of the group, had the honour of answering the questions and this time it didn't seem to upset me. I first told her what the Lampstead acronym of fine was: F = fucked up; I = insecure; N = neurotic; E = emotionally unstable.

She laughed at this, which pleased me. That quote has been drilled into my head every time I have said I was fine – well, it's either that or being told that the word "fine" isn't an emotion.

I was genuinely happy to help this lady with so many of her questions, and she seemed quite reassured and somewhat confident as she left the room. I hate to say it, but some of those quotes that the therapists repeat over and over again do work. It takes some time to mull it over in your head, but the sayings do get decrypted and analysed by the ever-changing mind.

I walk out of the door feeling satisfied, and I really hate to admit it, but I'm proud of myself. Even if the lady doesn't heed any of my advice, I know that I did my best. I may still be in here, but that doesn't mean I haven't learned a thing or two. I just don't think I'm ready to be truly helped yet.

12:00pm.

Lunch comes and goes while I lie curled up in my fluffy blanket. I like the combination of napping and watching TV, and I indulge over the next two hours. Strangely, no one comes to check on me during this time. Weird.

I know that I am not on general observations, thereby I only get checked on three times a day. I'm not complaining because I hate the checks, but I honestly feel a little let down, like they forgot about me.

Be realistic, Beth, and don't go down that road… It only leads to the dark scary place. The scary place may be comfortable but remember all those things you told that lady and use them on yourself. They probably did check but you may have been napping. I snap out of it and realize that it is time for a Diet Coke, a smoky treat, then arts and crafts with Grace and whoever else is around for the weekend.

On my way to the art room I start to get excited: I can already hear some hilarious conversations echoing through the hallways from my fellow arts and crafts members. I step inside and see five other patients plus Grace. I owe someone something for putting this odd mixture of people together. Normally I like to work on a puzzle with Grace because we both enjoy working on puzzles and I feel good completing something with her by my side, but this time I decide to grab a simple colouring template so I can listen in without having to concentrate too much.

First of all, we have Edwina spouting on about the horrors of Dr Bradley and what an undignified man he is, all while Grace is mending a tear in poor Julius. I think Grace is the only one Edwina allows to sew him up.

Next to them are two older gentlemen who I am sure are geniuses, but their intelligence caught up to them in this mad world. They are caught up in a very scientific conversation of which I am certainly not able to understand. I'm not an idiot but these two bring IQ and intelligence to a whole new level. It has something to do with time, space, gravity and a whole bunch of theories and equations. They are most certainly mad geniuses. It is often said that the more intelligent you are, the more likely you will suffer from some sort of mental illness.

Sitting next to them are another couple of lovely yet interesting patients. One is a woman who speaks in a very high, shrieky whisper. It is unknown to all of us whether or not to answer her questions or to ask her to repeat what she said. All she draws and paints are horses that are incredibly beautiful.

Next to her is a man colouring in a similar template of shapes as me. He seems to be in his own world because he is talking about fishing and doesn't even really care as to whether or not anyone listens. Every now and again I throw him a bone and comment on his soliloquy.

All of a sudden, a man wearing only a poncho – who I believe to be my age – walks in, grabs some tissue from the centre of the arts table and starts to chew it. He makes a circle around the table and grabs a few more sheets as he walks back out again and continues to chew. It phases me slightly, but as I said before, I'm used to this kind of thing, and, after all, he did offer me some extremely questionable "vodka" in my first days here… I am pretty sure it wasn't vodka, but my main concern is still why the *hell* did I take it? I had no idea who this person was, and I was in a completely new country and a completely new situation. He was actually one of the first people I encountered at Lampstead, and at first I wondered why in the hell I was in the same place as a disturbed, almost naked man running around the halls, but eventually I ended up loving him to death. Just to bring any thoughts about him to an end, we ended up becoming great friends and his "odd ways" are simply a case of his medication. He is still a dear friend whom I know I can talk to whenever I need to. He is truly an amazing person who is keen to help any and every one, and he is always looking for new ways to better others as well as himself and family.

This disturbance brings Edwina back to the present, leading her to question why she is in the same hospital as he is because she certainly isn't *that* crazy. She next turns her attention to the lady drawing horses and starts a conversation that soon turns into an argument. They both discuss their days of riding, but it soon turns heated as they compete about where they went to ride horses. It is as comical as you can imagine and I want to add in the fact that I have just had a horse named after me but decide it isn't really the right time. Edwina decides to take the last word, grabbing Julius as she walks out of the room and commenting very shrilly that she can't believe she is in here with all these fools and then tells the poor lady that she draws horses horribly. The lady must not have been too bothered about the argument because she starts talking about her medication and whether or not she should be given it.

I silently laugh, trying to keep it in, and Grace can definitely tell. Thankfully, one of my friends walks in the room and we start chatting and playing Scrabble. This is why I love Saturday arts and crafts. It brings out those who normally stay in their rooms and you seriously never know what is going to happen.

Sometime after 3:30pm.
All good things must come to an end and arts and crafts was finished for the day. As I walk out for a smoky treat – well a few smoky treats, I feel my mood drop slightly. *Ok, Bethany. This isn't the end of the world. You can do something else for the rest of the day. Who knows what is waiting for you in the next couple of hours!*

I want to believe my subconscious but it is really hard to. I know the right things to do. I know the right things to say but does it really matter in the long run if you can't feel them in your body? In your soul? I feel my heart start to break again. It is like the feeling of losing someone, and maybe that is exactly what it is. I am losing myself.

They say that in order to get "better" you have to sink to the bottom. I think I am very close to the bottom. *Bethany, snap out of it. You have to snap out of it right now. You are heading into a scary place. Whatever you do, think before you act. You can't act on any impulsive urges. Think of all the good of today. Think of all the good that will be. Get your ass out of this funk!*

I think I nap, but I'm not sure. Time is lost to me at the moment. I clearly dissociated. The TV is on, but I don't even register what is playing. I look at the clock. 7:30. *Shit. Why did you waste your day like that? What did you even do?* Well, that's an easy answer. There is nothing to waste. I am expendable. I am just one person taking up space and intruding on other people's lives.

Fuck it. I shouldn't be here in this world. I punch the wall once softly, then start pounding into it despite the pain and the swelling of my knuckles.

I hear a knock at the door. "Night staff… just checking on you."

I quickly shout through the door that I'm fine and I'll see them in a bit. They close the door again. I lose the momentum of my punches. I don't even feel the pain. I need something visible. Something that I can see. Something that makes me see what a horrid creature I am.

I find my piece of glass at the bottom of the tissue box and immediately go to town on my wrists and arms. I need to see the blood. There's no real reason to it other than to feel the pain, to see the blood and remind myself that I am not as good a person as people think. Why do so many people care about me?

Impulsivity is a weird thing. People may say they are impulsive, but most people don't impulsively try to kill themselves after having a fairly good morning and a tough evening. I'm impulsively reckless with myself and it is only later that I realize the consequences.

I try to stop the bleeding as much as I can, and I realize my cuts were only scratches. I don't want to get blood on anything in my room so I bandage my arm as best as possible. *What the fuck? You can't even manage to cut yourself deeply enough!*

I'm a failure. I can't even hurt myself properly. It bubbles in my chest, and I get even angrier with myself. I go into my closet and unearth the bottle of wine and bottles of beer I have stashed away. I find the many boxes of paracetamol and ibuprofen as well. I create one big pile of pills on my bed and open the wine. Without thinking, seven pills are gulped down. *Hang on a second, Bethany. Think. Where are you going with this? Stopping now isn't going to do any damage. But you are past the phase of not reporting it because there will be signs in the morning…*

I ignore the voice in my head. I can't believe how easy it was to just swallow seven pills with wine. I grab another handful and finish the wine. I open a beer and grab some more.

Darkness.

Someone checks my blood pressure and says it is extremely low.

Darkness.

I briefly open my eyes. I'm in a hospital bed with an IV stuck into my arm with several bags of fluids dripping into me.

Oh, shit…

Darkness.

PART TWO

LIFE BEYOND LAMPSTEAD

CHAPTER SEVEN

For some reason, mental health issues are much more difficult to communicate to others. Often, there are no words that are able to specifically define what is going on in a person's head. You can say you are "sad" or "angry" or even "happy", but what do those words actually mean? Different people have different definitions for those words. For one person, feeling sad could mean that their favourite restaurant has closed down. For another person being sad could mean that they are having a bad day and nothing seems to be going right for them at the moment. People are incredibly sad when loved ones die. These "sad" feelings are all completely relevant to the person declaring them, but it illustrates that "sad" means something different to different people. The word (among many other "feeling words") may be used too much for it to have a true meaning. Likewise, to one person, the word "upset" may not relate to how they're feeling, and the word "sad" would be more appropriate. The same is true vice-versa. And "upset" can even sometimes be the most appropriate word to define a certain sadness.

This is important when it comes to defining the word "depressed". The word "depressed" is frequently heard – people say it all the time: "I'm so depressed! I have nothing to do this weekend!" For a person who has a mental illness, "depressed" has a whole different meaning, and must be taken seriously. But how does one know which is which? Well, mental health depression is rarely verbally communicated, because not many sufferers know how to define true depression. This is when communication comes into play. Depression can be expressed in the way people act, or the things they say, or even the opposite – when they say nothing at all. People who are truly depressed often put on an "I'm fine mask", and are unwilling to say they are depressed. It is up to the people around them to figure out what is really going on. I once heard about a statistic that claimed one in five people are depressed (however, how deep these depressions are is not clear). Depression, and all of its accompanying symptoms, come in different forms. There may even be a depression gene. But, there is no discrimination in the ache, desperation and pure hopelessness of depression – whatever your race, gender, wealth, educational status, upbringing and so on. And it is this very range of manifestations and sufferers that makes it so difficult for professionals to treat those afflicted.

Despite my stories about some of the more interesting people I met, I also met so many more people at the hospital whom society would see as "normal". To an outsider, our lives seemed great. Some may even say perfect. There were extremely rich families, loving families with many kids, devoted couples, and people with wonderful jobs. The famous as well as the infamous. Millionaires as well as simple ex-housekeepers, like me. But as I said, it was the everyday type of person that held up the hospital – those with office jobs, or moms and dads, retirees, shopkeepers and so on… Many people on the outside just thought that they were going on a mini holiday to just get through some really rough times. Nevertheless, and disregarding what society and many family members thought of us, we still knew what was going on in our heads.

Family members don't always agree that there is a problem. They think the facade is the real person. Take Amy Winehouse, for example. People didn't think she needed help and the public made jokes about her, yet, in my opinion, she was crying out for some kind of intervention. Mental illness just doesn't sit well with society. It doesn't sit well with the hypocrites that think the mentally ill are taking money out of the system by being unable to work.

Yet, there is something comforting in being with those who understand what you are going through – that's what I found at Lampstead. I was allowed to mope about, but I was also allowed to have fun, which, having seen this someone on the outside would have said, "See! She is well! She is having fun! Why are we paying so much money if she isn't depressed and is having fun!"

What these people don't see is the agony going on in our heads, and we welcome the chance to share something together – even if it is a game that involves having fun. I can almost assure you that despite having fun, our issues were still at the forefront of our thoughts. At least mine were.

We are all good at masking the hopelessness. I'm sure that each and every one of us from Lampstead has at least one, if not many, fun moments and stories that we can take out into the real world to remind us that life isn't so bad. Many of my greatest stories (as well as my most heart-warming stories) have come from being there. So many times we took advantage of the fact that we were "mentally ill", and got as much out of it as we could. One Halloween a few of us stood outside the gate and seriously acted up being the stereotypical mental patient, which included fashioning straitjacket-type garments and headgear, and I am happy to say I probably freaked someone out. Sadly, we were told to go back inside. However, we still had glow necklaces that everyone – even the staff (especially Sheila) – enjoyed.

There were also always instances of, "Crap! I screwed up! Oh well, I'm mental." Those two words could almost apply to anything while in there – but of course you had to remember all of the stigma which is placed on mental patients outside the grounds. The fact of the matter is that we weren't "mental" in a bad, scary way. We were in some of the most horrible phases of our lives.

As I said though, it didn't prevent us from having fun. We were constantly playing board games and cards (warning: Monopoly still makes enemies of us all even in a psychiatric hospital!). We laughed and cried at movies as well as at daily and past events. Group therapy in the outside smoking hut without a therapist involved allowed patients to actually enjoy talking with those whom they found the most comfortable instead of those assigned to the group.

One of the best seasons that I was there for was the summer. So many people would go outside and lie on blankets or towels and take a nap, listen to music or just read. *Forget about the groups. It is gorgeous outside.* It was a thought that many of us had and it helped us all. Honestly, who can complain about people getting more vitamin D! People would go outside and play football or just throw a ball around. One year they also put up a badminton net and we just played until it got dark in our bare feet and would scream profanities when we missed the birdie. (FYI screaming helps!) At one point we had a ping-pong table set up in the "church" and I don't think that room has ever heard so many bad words!

It was always someone's birthday so there always seemed to be a movie or pizza party going on. We honestly cared about the people there and cared if they had some kind of special event happening in their lives.

There were puzzle "parties" and popcorn "parties" and ghost hunts at night. Scavenger hunts created by patients were a treat (I have to admit, people are still to this day talking about the one I created!). Think about it, who knows the hospital better than the patients? We are the only ones there 24/7! The best entertainment, almost always, came from the patients. Every now and then a nurse would try to create some kind of social event, but only we knew the mood of pretty much all of the patients and how likely we or others were to attend these events.

Sometimes it could seem like a really dull place, and I may have misled you into thinking so, but we did have some fun when we were in a good enough mood to leave our rooms. So, like those on the outside world, we too were able to have our exciting, angry or sad days. Ours just came at much more extreme levels.

So, what happened? Yeah, it was an unsuccessful suicide attempt. One of many that year. This one actually scared me though. It happened to be a somewhat accidental overdose that turned into an intentional overdose. After many mini overdoses and generally abusing myself, my body decided that it had had enough.

I don't really remember those days in the hospital other than being terrified, feeling awful and wondering what was going to happen to me. I never knew that taking so many painkillers would create such an intense amount of pain. It was also the first time that I realized I had made a huge mistake and was so incredibly happy to be alive. For three days, I was incredibly grateful.

I would love to say that a week or two later I discovered my turning point, but that wasn't to be the case. I soon almost forgot about what I did, and when I remembered it, it all seemed like a joke and that people were just trying to scare me by saying how close I had come to dying. To this day, I still don't know what saved me or what to make of the situation I put myself in, as well as so many others. The only thing I know for sure is that I can thank Shannon for finding me and also for sitting by my bedside in the middle of the night at the hospital, when I was breaking down and completely in tears.

One of the most awkward things about being such a high-risk patient at Lampstead was that once I got back from the hospital, I had to have a nurse with me 24/7, otherwise known as being on 1:1. I had absolutely no time to myself – especially in the beginning. I couldn't even be in the bathroom without the door being open a bit. Try doing your business or taking a shower with someone watching you. It is weird and quite disturbing. The first week of being on 1:1, my hygiene plummeted but my bowel movements did not. Thankfully, the second week I was allowed to have the bathroom door closed, though I was slightly bothered by them knocking on the door every three or five minutes. *Seriously? We all know there is nothing in the bathroom I can hurt myself with* (they took everything except the toilet paper out and I had to ask for anything else). The bathtub takes about thirty minutes to fill so it's not like I'm going to drown myself! I know all safety measures need to be taken so I do understand from the nursing side, but from the patient's perspective it feels downright rude!

Oh, and did I forget to mention the fact that they had to be in the room while I was sleeping? I would always turn my back to them so at least I didn't have to know whether they were staring at me intently. It is quite difficult to sleep knowing that someone you barely know is watching you. What was even more annoying is the fact that a few of the nurses needed light to supposedly write their notes when in fact they were reading a book or magazine. I couldn't care less about what they were doing, for heaven's sake! Let them watch a movie on their phone because sitting for several hours in the dark is not only as boring as hell, but I'm sure (and know for sure) that they must have fallen asleep as well.

It was great when I had nurses who I got on well with and we could talk about anything – serious or not. A lot of the time, I let them watch whatever they wanted on TV while I was doing something. The worst times were those when I had nurses who didn't know me or had no trust in me whatsoever, and if all I had to do was walk down the hall for a glass of water, they had to follow. If it was snowing or raining or downright freezing at whatever time of night, they still had to follow me down to the smoking area. I also felt really bad once we had made it downstairs to go to a group, and for whatever reason I forgot something back up in my room. They had to follow me back up. I heard many sighs and saw rolling eyes when I wanted to do anything other than sit on my bed, but sometimes sitting on my bed and watching TV was even worse because there were a few nurses who couldn't care less about what you were watching and continued to talk throughout the entire show or movie, no matter how much you tried to shut them up! In a way, I thought they would enjoy sitting down and relaxing, doing nothing other than watch some crappy TV for an hour or two, but nope. I had to hear all about their lives, the things going on around the hospital and the complaints about it all.

I also got a live commentary about whatever I was watching, like, "Wow, how can she be so stupid? Of course, he is going to go with the pretty one blah, blah, blah." There was also the occasional, "Oh, the ending to this movie is amazing! You never would have guessed that he would die in the last five minutes!" Well, there's that movie ruined!

In the beginning I used to care about pleasing my 1:1 nurse until I realized that it was their job. They were being paid to follow me around. After this lightbulb moment, I pretty much just did what I wanted to do and occasionally looked around to see if my shadow had caught up to me.

One time I had Katie as my nurse, and she was walking rather slowly to catch up with me. I quickly ran to the nursing station and hid. The nurses there thought it was hilarious and wanted in on the joke, so they played along by saying they had no idea where I was. I only let it go on for a few minutes because I could tell she was freaking out. It was around that time that they stopped giving me a shadow and I was off 1:1.

It might sound weird, but the first night alone without anyone in my room freaked me out a bit. I had gotten used to someone watching over me like a mini security guard. Other than that though, I was super happy to be on my own, and my friends at the time were also happy for me not to have a shadow because in a way they were also scrutinized by whoever was on my tail that day while I was in the group.

CHAPTER EIGHT

A week in Lampstead Hospital can feel like a lifetime.
For some, you enter and never leave… Luckily for
me, my "week" during that admission lasted for
nine months. After three admissions and millions
of money that my insurance paid, it was eventually
decided that my funding was to run out. This was
my one fear that I lived with on a day-to-day basis,
always lingering at the back of my mind. I knew that
my insurance wouldn't last forever but I never really
believed that it would actually happen before I was
truly ready (would I ever be ready?)…

My therapist, as well as everyone else, knew three
days before I found out, but they didn't want to
tell me as the day they found out was my birthday.
"Happy Birthday! And by the way, you have to
leave tomorrow." Somehow they managed to get the
hospital or insurance company to pay for a few more
days – I really don't want to know the specifics, but
all I could think of once I'd found out was that I had
to abandon my "home" and go into a world in which
I really knew nothing. I was a 29-year-old with the
mindset of a 12-year-old. "Who is going to take care

of me now?" was my biggest question, along with "How do I live without this odd family, safety and routine I have created?" Every single staff member seemed to be asking the same questions, but they mostly centred around one deadly question: "Will she live through the week of not being here?" They were still concerned about my suicide attempt, when death was so near the door to me that everyone felt it… so, yeah, their fears were well founded. I wouldn't be here to write this story had some kind of miracle, divine intervention or whatever you want to call it not happened.

Little did I know that, oddly enough, the cards were playing in my favour and I was about to face my very first challenge in "real" life. If I can live life outside of the hospital, then there may be a chance that I could survive in general… for a month at the least.

There must be someone or something out there who has been watching over me, even when situations have seemed dire (not only to me but to others as well – just to prove I'm not looking at the negative!). I must be like Cinderella or some other Disney princess and have an invisible fairy godmother looking out for me, saving my ass.

Most of the time I am incredulous and feel as if I don't deserve all the luck and care that has been given to me. I feel like I need to do more to earn the aid. My parents, along with many, many staff members, saved me at this crucial end to a long affair with Lampstead. I was to have a live-in nurse for a month or so. How did this sudden development pop up, and how was I able to find the perfect, furnished two-bedroom flat, which was so close to the hospital that I still felt comfortable within a week? To be honest, I still have no idea. Things just happened to work out in my favour.

So many people were involved in my transfer out of Lampstead. I owe this mostly to two people: Dr Ramsey (my main psychiatrist) and Dr C. I had never really had a proper conversation with Dr C before, but Ramsey wanted a second opinion on my situation and so he entered my world. I don't even know how to describe him other than passionate for his work, down to earth and incredibly talented. When you speak with him you forget that you are speaking with a very prominent psychiatrist and instead you have a normal conversation.

He didn't have to stay as a part of my team, but for some reason he said that he would love the opportunity. He even told me that there was something special about me and that I intrigued him. Those words, and the fact that he stuck by me through thick and thin, were probably the first compliments I let sink in. He was the one to arrange the in-home treatment. I had extreme doubts and if I had been in my "right" mind and not overwhelmed about what would happen to me, I may have said no. But the important thing for me to realize was that I trusted him despite my trust issues. I put my life in his hands. This is actually a major compliment to him as I don't trust people easily!

I was weirded out at first and terrified of living with a stranger who was completely in control of everything to do with my life (even out of the hospital), but there was no way of getting out of it.

Luckily, I was assigned two of the most inspirational, caring, strict (yet fun) nurses whom I am sure saved my life several times. They also served as a transition back into society, as well as a "friend" to talk to. Actually, to this day, I'd still consider them more my friends than my nurses, though I'm not allowed to be in contact with them. This fact alone pains me almost more than the thought of someone you barely know, because when you live with someone 24/7 and they know all your secrets and can read you like a book (that is their job after all!) a bond is created. A friendship is quickly formed – it has to be, otherwise there is no reason to pay for a private nurse.

I grew into my "real-world self" with them by my side. They were there for me for whatever I needed, whenever I needed it. I don't think I really realized this until the last few weeks that I had them by my side.

Now that I've been discharged from their care, I'm not even able to send a text saying, "Hi! How's it going?" I can't tell them some crazy story that happened to me and I'm especially not allowed to know how things are going with them.

Knowing that they are out there but having no means to contact them takes a lot of life out of me. They may have been strict, but I loved them – their crazy stories and how we laughed at everything, even the tears I shed on their shoulders. Don't we all remember that I have major abandonment issues?! But it's not to be. I can't consider it abandonment this time: they are professionals and I knew that this would come to an end at some point. I just didn't know that I would care so much! They helped me, and I'd love to think that I may have helped them in some ways, too. I'll never know, but you don't always know everything in life, do you? If I were to name ten people who were most influential in my life, their names would be among them.

When I first moved out of Lampstead and started living with them, I didn't think I would make it. I don't think even they thought I would. In my opinion, I believe that they thought they were just wasting their time to get me to want a new life. To want more for myself. To dream for myself, to save myself. While writing this, I can say that it has been hard work – harder than anything I think I have had to do, but everything has started to sink in.

It is weird to think that several months ago two strangers entered my world, my little bubble, knowing so much about me and I had no clue as to what I was getting myself into. All I know is that I was given plenty of lorazepam and diazepam during this period to keep me from completely freaking out.

Well, I do know one thing. They didn't know everything about me! The first question one of the nurses asked their supervisor was if she was in any danger of me hurting her. I still chuckle about this because I'd hurt myself in a second before hurting others. Neither of them knew how stubborn I am and unwilling to get better. I was so used to hating myself and feeling only misery that I was too scared to try out this whole "better" thing. Let's just say they had their work cut out for them.

I think most of their work was mainly trying not to get too angry with me and completely give up. They could talk to me until they were blue in the face, and yes, I would listen, but at the same time I would be creating a subconscious counter-argument in my head.

I wanted them to believe me. I am, after all, a people pleaser. I wanted them to think I was doing well, but it was all an act − a very expensive act that I put on for about two and a half months. I don't think that time was wasted though. I needed people not to play into my games; I needed them to make me feel horrible about myself in order to see the truth. Life itself isn't a game. Well it is, but you are playing it only with yourself. Others will get tired and leave.

On one occasion, after I was being stupid about something, one of the nurses calmed me down and confessed it had been the first time she had ever yelled at anyone in her life. Something in my head started to turn after that – some little gear that started to change the way I think.

Through many arguments and battles, they taught me that even though I have mental health issues, I can do things to help myself. I don't have to wallow selfishly in my own head. I do have the choice to be happy – not every day, mind you – but some days I can choose, and I do have the strength to get through it. Once I let myself go and fall into their care, I was finally able to start taking in what they were saying. Things like how the mind and body work, how everything I put into my body (or don't) affects logic, that I do have the ability to be a "normal" person and that I am making myself feel like a failure. I've spent too much time dredging up the past and worrying about the future that I am missing out on this moment – a moment that could be horrible or wonderful, but nevertheless it is the only moment I have control over and it's the only one I need to focus on. Everything changes. I can't help that, though I wish I could!

Therefore, they taught me that I am capable of changing with everything because I do have those skills. They didn't waste their time, but sadly nothing they or anyone else said or did only sank in until the very end of my time with them. They were my "paid for" resources and I failed to use them.

I will be starting my MSc in Psychology in the autumn, and if I can't help myself, how am I supposed to help others? A simple concept, I know, but to someone who has had no desires, felt hopeless and alone, and worthless for close to 29 years, it is easy to understand but harder to put into place. I still have my absolutely shitty days where I may slip up a bit, but at least I have the knowledge that tomorrow or next week may be better. I'd like to believe that the best therapists out there have either had some kind of hardship themselves, or they have been close to someone who has. I'd also like to believe that my experiences would be of some benefit to someone. Who knows better than me about what it feels like to cut your arm or taking too many meds that you end up unconscious and in the hospital?

CHAPTER NINE

The days seem to go on forever, but the nights never have enough time in them. Nights are the hardest, but oddly the easiest to deal with. Today marks four months of being out of the hospital and every day is different. I wake up with different moods – some days I call in sick to work and stay in bed the whole day (right now I'm just volunteering at a shop), but other days I bound out of bed, have my coffee and a cigarette out on the balcony, clean my rabbit's cage and leave my apartment early in the day, either for work or exploring. I can honestly say that I have no idea which Bethany I will wake up to, especially since my nights differ as well. So many hours of the night have been spent sitting on my balcony, having a glass (or bottle) of wine and thinking about hurting or even killing myself while watching interesting people walk strangely down the street. These nights are completely unproductive and the opposite of all the support and treatment that my family has given me.

Sometimes I act upon the least bad voices, such as just scratching or burning myself, or I continue to drink that whole bottle of wine because no one is going to be hurt except myself. I normally end up falling asleep on the sofa and getting little to no sleep. Other nights, I sit in that state for a little bit, then my mind opens up and ideas spring into my head. *I should be cleaning! I need to finish my book! I need to start some laundry and whatever mundane yet positive distraction I can think of.*

With either choice – neither being good, because both situations end up with me staying up too late and still having dangerous thoughts – I'm still exhausted the next day. Even at this point in my life, the next day still intimidates me for some reason. I have no idea what it will bring. It must just be the unknown, or the fact that I've either wasted a day of life in a good or bad sense. The fact that I am even writing these words at 1:30am worries me. What am I living for that may or may not happen tomorrow? There is nothing planned. Life goes on and nothing special happens. I know this sounds naïve, but shouldn't there be something in my future to look forward to? Shouldn't there be someone on the other line of the phone for me to call and just chat about nothing in particular – or even see if they want to go out for a drink? Fuck. Life is hard.

I almost envy the days when people's life spans were no longer than 30. I know that this is a common feeling (or at least a topic that has been brought up), so it's not like I am saying anything new. I have no new news to share with anyone. I am the same boring person you started off reading the book about – at least that Bethany had some spunk! She could be sarcastic and still learn and feel important.

Out in the "real world", I am nobody. That is pretty much my story. Nothing "bad" ever happened to me. I was never raped or abused or even had anyone close to me die. I'm just your average 30-year-old with a lot of stupid emotional baggage that I feel many people can relate to. Not everyone has gotten the support I have, and although I am not religious, I do feel blessed. Someone or something has been looking out for me.

So many people have entered my life in the past three or four years who have saved me – literally saved my life. I'm so overwhelmed with thankfulness as well as a bit of embarrassment because, although most don't agree with me, I have nothing special to give. Maybe not everyone experiences that, but those that have understand. I know for a fact that they face the moment when reality kicks them in the face and they finally see that people honestly care.

It's cliché, I know. People do come in and out of your life, but you don't always know the reason. I was lucky in the fact that those who care about me suddenly came out of the woodwork and I was able to finally understand. It may have taken almost 30 years, but it happened. Every night when I sit on that balcony and think how best to hurt myself or end everything completely, I think about those who care. I used to think you had to be a strong person to kill yourself, but really, I think it is for the confused and not the selfish, as many people say. They have yet to see the care of others and the effects it will cause.

Still, as is true for me (I'm not taking myself out of that category quite yet!), it is a choice. A choice only one person can make. Put the armour on and face the dark forces alone, or allow the rest of your troop of warriors in to help end the battle. There is always a choice and always the fight, but now I have somewhat of a safety net of people who existed and somehow knew me even before I knew them.

Friends aren't your only resource: others will come into your life as strangers and somehow change your perspective, even if it is only for a minute. That minute counts. That is one minute out of the rest of the hours of the day that you felt a sense of pride, being needed or even a small act that gave you a positive feeling, like helping someone pick up something they dropped. Every little thing helps, and the moment you can see that is the same moment that you see a glimpse of possibility.

Don't get me wrong, I ain't preaching! It's hard work – especially when you are so focused inwardly (which is ok). Let it happen on its own. It's taken me

30 years and I think I may have about 10 cracks in my egg, but with every crack, it becomes easier and easier to break the shell and see what is beneath. Everyone has a favourite quote or saying, and I think I must have about 50 million of them, but one saying written by Nietzsche sticks with me. Sarah read it to us in drama therapy back in my early days at Lampstead, and it has stuck with me since and always makes me think. In one of his books called *The Gay Science* he writes, *"What, if some day or night a demon were to steal after you into your loneliest loneliness and say to you: 'This life as you now live it and have lived it, you will have to live once more and innumerable times more.' ... Would you not throw yourself down and gnash your teeth and curse the demon who spoke thus? Or have you once experienced a tremendous moment when you would have answered him: 'You are a god and never have I heard anything more divine.'"*

Well? What do you think? Only you have the answer. As my genius movement therapist Nick would say: "Where do we go from here?"

ACKNOWLEDGEMENTS

I obviously couldn't include every person in this book
that I wanted to, as so many people have influenced
my life. If I were to write the entire story of my life,
you would probably be reading (or paging through) a
book as long as the entire encyclopaedia. First of all,
thank you to Cherish Editions and Trigger Publishing
for taking me aboard and allowing my voice to be
heard. I want to thank my team in Italy, Jillian and
Sidney, as they were the ones who first took me fully
into their hands and ensured that I got the best
treatment possible (meaning they went above and
beyond to help me, as well as get me to the hospital).
Thanks as well to my family and everyone else at the
hospital, especially all my one to one therapists. You
gave me strength, and although I may have been
a pain in your ass (to patients as well as staff!), you
helped me. You all know who you are – especially if
we ever hugged. The quote below is one that I often
think of and feel is more relevant now than ever:

Psychotherapist Virginia Satir once said,
"We need 4 hugs a day for survival. We need

8 hugs a day for maintenance. We need 12 hugs a day for growth."

You all will be in my heart forever, and I may not have named you, but just know that you are not forgotten. As long as I am here, you will be with me as well. As the old cliché goes, despite whether you are near or far from me, "distance makes the heart grow fonder". Thank you all for keeping me alive. My life at the moment could have ended with a period, or as they say in England, a "full stop" but because of all of you, there is a semicolon. Life may stop at times, but you can make it continue (;) you have the choice to change it… Love to you all.

ABOUT CHERISH EDITIONS

Cherish Editions is a bespoke self-publishing service for authors of mental health, wellbeing and inspirational books.

As a division of Trigger Publishing, the UK's leading independent mental health and wellbeing publisher, we are experienced in creating and selling positive, responsible, important and inspirational books, which work to de-stigmatize the issues around mental health and improve the mental health and wellbeing of those who read our titles.

Founded by Adam Shaw, a mental health advocate, author and philanthropist, and leading psychologist Lauren Callaghan, Cherish Editions aims to publish books that provide advice, support and inspiration. We nurture our authors so that their stories can unfurl on the page, helping them to share their uplifting and moving stories.

Cherish Editions is unique in that a percentage of the profits from the sale of our books goes directly to leading mental health charity Shaw Mind, to deliver its vision to provide support for those experiencing mental ill health.

Find out more about Cherish Editions by visiting cherisheditions.com
or by joining us on:
Twitter @cherisheditions
Facebook @cherisheditions
Instagram @cherisheditions

Cherish
EDITIONS

ABOUT SHAWMIND

A proportion of profits from the sale of all Trigger books go to their sister charity Shawmind, also founded by Adam Shaw and Lauren Callaghan. The charity aims to ensure that everyone has access to mental health resources whenever they need them.

You can find out more about the work Shaw Mind do by visiting their website: shawmind.org or joining them on

Twitter @Shaw_Mind
Facebook @ShawmindUK
Instagram @Shaw_Mind

Lightning Source UK Ltd.
Milton Keynes UK
UKHW040654030621
384828UK00001B/131